The Christian Handbook

## About the Smiling Fish

The icon of the "Smiling Fish" on the cover reminds us of the importance of good Christian humor. The "ichthus" or fish symbol for Christ was used by early Christians as a secret way to express their faith. Like the early Christians, the place of humor in the Christian life is sometimes misunderstood by the outside world. The "Smiling Fish" corrects this misunderstanding and suggests our need to make humor an important part of our witness to Christ.

# The Christian Handbook

MINNEAPOLIS

THE CHRISTIAN HANDBOOK HANDBOOK

Copyright © 2005 Augsburg Fortress. All rights reserved. Except for brief quotations in critical articles or reviews, no part of this book may be reproduced in any manner without prior written permission from the publisher. Write to: Permissions, Augsburg Fortress, Box 1209, Minneapolis, MN 55440.

Scripture quotations are from the *Holy Bible, New International Version®*, copyright © 1973, 1978, 1984 by International Bible Society. Used by permission of Zondervan Publishing House. All rights reserved. The "NIV" and "New International Version" trademarks are registered in the United States Patent and Trademark Office by International Bible Society. Use of either trademark requires the permission of International Bible Society.

Sources for the charts on pages 56–61 include reference materials from *Information Please®*, New York Times Public Library/Hyperion, Rose Publishing, Time-Life, and Wadsworth Group/Thomas Learning.

Editor: Kristofer Skrade
Cover designer: Laurie Ingram-Duren
Production editor: James Satter
Interior illustrator: Brenda Brown

ISBN 0-8066-5259-4

The paper used in this publication meets the minimum requirements of American National Standard for Information Sciences—Permanence of Paper for Printed Library Materials, ANSI Z329.48-1984.

Manufactured in the U.S.A.

09   08   07   06   05           1   2   3   4   5   6   7   8   9   10

# CONTENTS

*Charts and Diagrams*

# Everyday Stuff

# Bible Stuff                                                        131

# PREFACE

## *Please Be Advised:*

Lots of books and pamphlets have appeared through the centuries as companions for average folks who needed help navigating their way through a complicated subject. *The American Red Cross First Aid and Safety Handbook* comes to mind, for example. So does *National Audubon Society's Field Guide to North American Reptiles and Amphibians.* There are even handbooks to unusual subjects like UFO's, cryptozoology, and crop circles, to name a few. And even if you never intend to bandage a head wound, identify a *Chilomeniscus cinctus* in the wild, or search for bigfoot, you can still gain something valuable by reading those books. You can learn something.

Books like these stand as testimony to the need of average people for a guide to the vast truths and intricate detail of something unfamiliar to them. Or, the subject may not be completely unfamiliar to them; they may just want reliable, written information and clear diagrams or drawings they can refer to easily, in a pinch. (Even the most seasoned ornithologists carry handbooks with them so they can be sure they've actually seen the first Blue-faced Booby or Red-whiskered Bulbul of the season!)

*The Christian Handbook* is a combination survival guide, field guide, and handbook for people in need of some basic information or people looking for a handy companion to which they can refer anytime. Here you will discover a combination of reliable historical and theological information alongside some fun (and funny) facts and some very practical tips on being a churchgoing follower of Jesus Christ, all presented in a down-to-earth, tongue-in-cheek sort of way. Humor, after all, is the most often forgotten—but one of the most important—ingredients in a healthy faith life.

Anyway, the point is that being a follower of Jesus is hard enough without having to navigate the faith journey—let alone the maze of Christian church culture—all alone. Sooner or later everyone needs a companion.

—THE EDITOR

# *CHURCH STUFF*

Every well-prepared churchgoer should have a basic understanding of Christian teachings and where they came from. Plus, since every church goes about worship in a slightly different way, it might take a little time to get the hang of things—especially if you're new to a congregation.

This section includes:

- Essential facts about the Christian faith. (If you know these things, you'll know more than most.)
- Practical advice for singing hymns, staying alert, and getting to know the people in your church.
- Hints for enjoying worship—even when you're having a bad day.

# HOW TO FIND A CHURCH

Whether you're looking for a church for the first time, have decided to join a different congregation, or have moved to a new town, locating a faith community is an important part of your life as a Christian.

**❶ Pray.**
Ask the Holy Spirit to guide you on your search for a church home.

**❷ List your priorities.**
When you feel you've got a handle on it, make a list of your criteria for your new church and prioritize it. Determine "must have" requirements versus "nice-to-have" extras.

**❸ Solicit advice from friends, coworkers, and relatives in the area.**
Trusted friends and family members can suggest congregations you can visit. Ask to accompany them to their own place of worship.

**❹ Use the Internet and browse local phone directories.**
Perform an online search for churches in your area or look up "churches" in the business listings of your phone book. Many churches have a homepage featuring their worship service schedules, contact information, directions, staff directories, and ministry opportunities.

**❺ Listen for bells and singing on Sunday mornings. Look for steeples. Keep an eye out for well-dressed or awake-looking people.**
Many churches ring loud bells at the beginning of worship services. The sound of a large group singing is also a good sign that a church may be nearby.

Church buildings can often be seen from a distance due to large bell towers and tall spires topped by crosses. Churchgoers sometimes don "Sunday clothes" for church and are often alert due to worship activity, typically more so following worship.

**⑥ Research the beliefs and practices of congregations you visit.**
Inform yourself as to the values and theological positions of the churches you visit. Make sure you share (or tolerate) those views before committing to join the congregation.

*Look for steeples as clues to guide you to a church.*

*Congregations often meet in houses, school gymnasiums, and other "nontraditional" buildings.*

**7** Visit a variety of churches with different environments.
Expose yourself to congregations that are both large and small, formal and informal, new and established.

**8** Determine how welcome you feel. Typically, the more the better.
Evaluate the church's response to your presence. Did the pastor greet you? Were you noticed by other worshipers? Did you meet anyone personally? Did anyone ask your name? Did this cause you to panic, or did it make you feel accepted?

## Be Aware

- If you join a church within walking distance or a short drive from your home, you'll be more likely to attend during busy times or in bad weather. Consider starting your search close to home.

- Many congregations meet in "nontraditional" buildings, such as theaters, warehouses, and school gymnasiums.

- No church is perfect.

# HOW TO GET TO KNOW YOUR PASTOR

Pastors play an important role in the daily life of your church and the community. Despite their godly profession, fancy robes, and knowledge of the Bible, pastors experience the same ups and downs as everyone else. They value people's efforts to meet, connect with, and support them.

**❶ Connect with your pastor after church.**

After the service, join the line to shake the pastor's hand. Sharing a comment about the sermon lets the pastor know his or her preparation time is appreciated. If your congregation doesn't practice the dismissal line, find other ways to make that personal connection on Sunday morning.

**❷ Pray daily for your pastor. Pastors don't just work on Sunday.**

Your pastor has many responsibilities, like visiting members in the hospital, writing sermons, and figuring out who can help drain the flooded church basement. In your prayers, ask God to grant your pastor health, strength, and wisdom to face the many challenges of leading a congregation.

**❸ Ask your pastor to share with you why he entered the ministry.**

There are many reasons why a pastor may have chosen to become a minister. Be prepared for a story that may surprise you.

**4** Stop by your pastor's office to talk, or consider making an appointment to get acquainted.

Pastors welcome the opportunity to connect with church members at times other than worship. As you would with any drop-in visit, be sensitive to the fact that your pastor may be quite busy. A scheduled appointment just to chat could provide a welcome break in your pastor's day.

*Getting to know your pastor can help you to get more out of church.*

# HOW TO SURVIVE FOR ONE HOUR IN AN UN-AIR-CONDITIONED CHURCH

Getting trapped in an overheated sanctuary is a common churchgoing experience. The key is to minimize your heat gain and electrolyte loss.

**❶ Plan ahead.**
When possible, scout out the sanctuary ahead of time to locate optimal seating near fans or open windows. Consider where the sun will be during the worship service and avoid sitting under direct sunlight. Bring a bottle of water for each person in your group.

**❷ Maintain your distance from others.**
Human beings disperse heat and moisture as a means of cooling themselves. An average-size person puts off about as much heat as a 75-watt lightbulb. The front row will likely be empty and available.

**❸ Remain still.**
Fidgeting will only make your heat index rise.

*Use your bulletin as a personal fan to keep cool.*

**❹ Think cool thoughts.**
Your mental state can affect your physical disposition. If the heat distracts you from worship, imagine you're sitting on a big block of ice.

**❺ Dress for survival.**
Wear only cool, breathable fabrics.

**❻ Avoid acolyte or choir robes when possible.**
Formal robes are especially uncomfortable in the heat. If you must wear one, make sure to wear lightweight clothes underneath.

**❼ Pray.**
Jesus survived on prayer in the desert for 40 days. Lifting and extending your arms in an open prayer position may help cool your body by dispersing excess heat. If you've been perspiring, though, avoid exposing others to your personal odor.

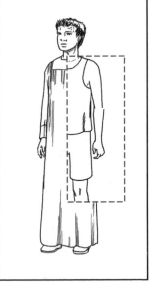

*On hot days, wear light clothing underneath acolyte or choir robes.*

## Be Aware

- Carry a personal fan—or use your bulletin as a substitute.
- Worship services scheduled for one hour sometimes will run long. Plan ahead.

# HOW TO RESPOND WHEN SOMEONE SITS IN YOUR PEW

We all carry a bubble of personal space. For some people, it's several feet. For others, it's about a millimeter. Wherever on the spectrum you happen to fall, there are certain situations in which we invite visitors into our little sphere of experience—like at church. Furthermore, human beings are territorial in nature and sometimes see strangers inside the bubble as an affront. These situations need not be cause for alarm.

**❶ Smile and greet the "intruders."**
Oftentimes they are visitors to your congregation—new blood. Avoid creating bad blood you might regret later on. Make solid eye contact so they know you mean it, shake hands with them, and leave no impression that they've done something wrong.

**❷ View the "intrusion" as an opportunity.**
Remember, you don't own the pew; you just borrow it once a week. Take the opportunity to get out of your rut and sit someplace new. This will physically emphasize a change in your perspective and may yield new spiritual discoveries.

**❸ If you can tell that your new friends feel uncomfortable at having displaced you, despite your efforts to the contrary, make an extra effort to welcome them.**
Consider taking them to brunch after church to become acquainted. If there are too many for you to foot the bill, consider inviting them to accompany you on a "go Dutch" basis. This will eliminate any hierarchy and place you on equal footing.

# HOW TO USE A WORSHIP BULLETIN

Some churches offer a printed resource called a bulletin to assist worshipers. The bulletin may contain the order of the service, music listings, Bible readings, and important community announcements.

**1** **Arrive early.**
A few extra minutes before worship will allow you to scan the bulletin and prepare for the service.

**2** **Receive the bulletin from the usher.**
Upon entering the worship space, an usher will give you a bulletin. Some churches stack bulletins near the entrance for self-service.

**3** **Review the order of worship.**
When seated, open the bulletin and find the order of the service, usually printed on the first or second page. Some churches print the entire service in the bulletin so worshipers don't have to switch back and forth between worship aids.

**4** **Determine if other worship resources are required.**
The order of worship may specify additional hymnals, Bible passages, song sheets, or other external supplies required during the service, or it may direct your attention to a projection screen.

**❺** Fill out the attendance card.

A card may be located inside the bulletin or somewhere in your row. Fill it out completely. You may be asked to pass this card to an usher or to place it in the offering plate. Some congregations have visitors/communion attendance books for people to sign.

**❻** Reflect on any bulletin artwork.

Covers often feature a drawing or design that corresponds to the season of the church year or the day's Bible verses. Examine the artwork and make a note of its connection to the sermon.

**❼** Track your worship progress.

The bulletin will guide you through the service, hymns or songs, and sermon time as you worship and let you know where you are at all times.

**❽** Identify the pastor(s), worship leaders, and assistants.

The names of ushers, musicians, greeters, readers, and the pastor(s) usually can be found in the bulletin. Greet these people by name following the service. Make good eye contact.

**❾** Review any printed announcements.

Community activities, church calendars, and updates are often listed in the back of the bulletin. Scan listings during down times or pauses in the service.

**❿** Make good use of the bulletin after the service.

Some churches re-use bulletins for later services. Return the bulletin if possible. Recycling bins may also be provided. If you wish, or unless otherwise instructed, you may take the bulletin home with you.

## Be Aware

- Bulletins often use letter or color codes to signify whether any hymnals should be used. Look for a key or legend that details this information.

- Many church offices and worship teams need help preparing the bulletin each week. You may want to volunteer to copy, fold, or assemble the bulletin for an upcoming service.

*If you choose not to save your worship bulletin, be sure to recycle it whenever possible.*

# HOW TO SING A HYMN

Music is an important part of the Christian tradition and an enjoyable way to build community. Hymn singing can be done without demonstrable emotion, but many otherwise stoic Christians appropriately channel emotion into their hymn singing and are therefore loud.

**❶ Locate hymns in advance.**
As you prepare for worship, consult the worship bulletin or the hymn board to find numbers for the day's hymns. Bookmark these pages in the hymnal using an offering envelope or attendance card.

**❷ Familiarize yourself with the hymns.**
Examine the composer credits, the years the composer(s) lived, and whether the tune has a different name than the hymn itself. Note how the hymn is categorized in the hymnal.

**❸ Assist nearby visitors or children.**
Using a hymnal can be confusing. If your neighbor seems disoriented, help them find the correct pages, or let them read from your book.

**❹ Adopt a posture for best vocal performance.**
Hold the hymnal away from your body at chest level. Place one hand under the spine of the binding, leaving the other hand free to turn the pages. Keep your chin up so your voice projects outward.

**❺ Begin singing.**
If the hymn is unfamiliar, sing the melody for the first verse. If you read music, explore the written harmony parts during the remaining verses. Loud-singing neighbors may or may not be in tune, so follow them with caution.

*Support the hymnal's spine with one hand. Place the other on the open page.*

**❻ Focus on the hymn's content.**
Some of the lyrics may connect with a Bible reading of the day. Certain ones may be especially inspiring.

**❼ Avoid dreariness.**
Hymns are often sung in such a serious way that the congregation forgets to enjoy the music. Sing with energy and feeling.

## Be Aware

- Hymnals are not just for use at church. Consider keeping a personal copy of a favorite hymnal at home for further reference and study. Hymnals also make excellent gifts.

- Some hymns use words and phrases that are difficult to understand (such as, "Here I raise my Ebenezer," from the hymn "Come, Thou Fount of Every Blessing"). Use a dictionary or a Bible with a concordance to clear up any uncertainty.

# HOW TO SING A PRAISE SONG

Many Christian congregations use modern worship styles, often called Praise & Worship (P&W), featuring guitars and drums. In these settings the words are often displayed on large, multimedia projection screens.

**❶ Follow the instructions of the song leader.**
Someone in the praise band will invite the congregation to stand up, sit down, repeat certain sections, or divide into men's and women's vocal parts. Pay attention to this person to avoid getting off track.

**❷ Learn the melody and song structure.**
Pay special attention to the melody line sung by the band's lead vocalist. Praise & Worship songs can be tricky because they are rarely printed with notated sheet music and are sung differently from place to place.

**❸ Sing along with gusto.**
Once the melody has been introduced, join in the singing. When you're comfortable with the song, experiment with harmony parts.

**❹ Avoid "zoning out."**
Singing lyrics that are projected on giant screens can result in a glazed-over facial expression. Avoid this by surveying the worship area and making eye contact with other people.

**❺ Identify lyrical themes.**
Determine if the song is being used as a confession, a prayer, a hymn of praise, or another purpose.

**⑥ Watch out for raised hands.**
Some Christians emote while singing contemporary
Christian songs and may suddenly raise their hands in
praise to God. Be sure to give these worshipers plenty of
room to avoid losing your eyeglasses.

## Be Aware

- Christian worship is highly participatory. The praise
  band is there to help you to sing and participate in
  worship, not to perform a concert.

- There are no strict prohibitions in the Christian tradition against physical expression during worship.

- In some congregations, praise gestures will draw amused
  stares; in others, NOT gesturing will draw amused stares.

*Beware of especially passionate worshipers
who might raise their hands too quickly.*

# HOW TO LISTEN TO A SERMON

Christians believe that God's Word comes to us through the Holy Spirit, the gospel of Jesus Christ, and the preaching of Holy Scripture. Getting something out of church includes diligent listening to the sermon and active mental participation.

 **Review active listening skills.**

While the listener in this case doesn't get to speak, the sermon is still a conversation. Make mental notes as you listen. Take notice of where and why you react and which emotions you experience.

❷ **Take notes.**

Note-taking promotes active listening and provides a good basis for later reflection. It also allows you to return to confusing or complicated parts at your own leisure. Some churches provide paper for notes.

❸ **Maintain good posture. Avoid slouching.**

Sit upright with your feet planted firmly on the ground and your palms on your thighs. Beware of the impulse to slouch, cross your arms, or lean against your neighbor, as these can encourage drowsiness.

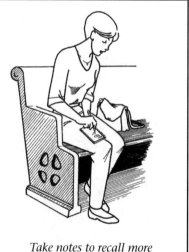

*Take notes to recall more information and get more out of the sermon.*

**❹ End by saying, "Amen."**
Since preaching is mostly God's work, honor the Word by sealing the moment with this sacred word.

**❺ Review.**
If you've taken written notes, read through them later that day or the next day and consider corresponding with the preacher if you have questions or need clarification.

If you've taken mental notes, review them in a quiet moment. Consider sharing this review time with others in your church or household on a weekly basis.

## Be Aware

- You may cry tears of joy during the sermon, or you may experience a feeling of conviction. This is normal.

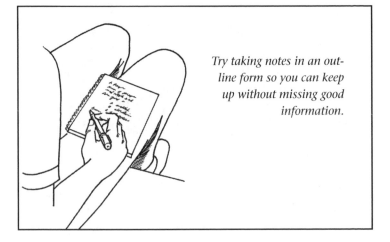

*Try taking notes in an outline form so you can keep up without missing good information.*

# HOW TO RESPOND TO A DISRUPTION DURING CHURCH

Disruptions during church are inevitable. The goal is to soften their impact.

**❶ Simply ignore the offending event, if possible.**
Many disruptions are brief and the persons involved act quickly to quiet them. Avoid embarrassing others; maintain your attention on the worship activity.

**❷ Some disruptions cannot be ignored and may threaten to continue indefinitely. The agony will go on unless you act. Consider the following types:**

### Active Children

- *Your Problem:* You are most familiar with your own family. If you sense an outburst will end quickly, simply allow it to pass. If not, escort the child to the lobby for a little quiet time, then return.

*Try to ignore worship interruptions you think will end soon.*

*Note:* Under all circumstances, children should be made to feel welcome in worship!

- *Someone Else's Problem:* Politely offer to help, perhaps by helping to occupy the child quietly or by escorting parent and tot to the lobby, nursery, or cry room.

### Personal Electronics

- *Your Problem:* Turn off cell phones, pagers, and other electronic alarms immediately and discreetly. If contact is made and it is critical, remove yourself to the lobby and call back. Under no circumstances should you answer your phone during worship.

*Turn off all personal electronic devices before worship.*

- *Someone Else's Problem:* Politely ask them to respect worship by moving the conversation to the lobby.

### Chatty Neighbor

- *Your Problem:* Chatty persons should be alert to stares and grim looks from neighbors and be prepared to stop talking upon seeing them.

- *Someone Else's Problem:* Politely ask the talkers to wait until after worship to conclude the conversation. During the coffee hour, approach them with a cookie to mend any offense they may have felt.

### Cameras

- *Your Problem:* Ask first if cameras are allowed. If so, unobtrusively and discreetly position yourself out of the line of sight of other worshipers. Be aware of the film's exposure number to avoid jarring auto-rewind noises. Flash cameras are strictly taboo.

- *Someone Else's Problem:* Politely offer to show the photographer where to stand to get the shot without obstructing worship.

### Sound System Feedback

- Pastors and worship leaders often make jokes to cover for feedback and keep the appropriate mood for worship. If this happens, consider making a donation earmarked for a "new sound system" in the offering plate.

# HOW TO PASS THE PLATE

Passing the offering plate requires physical flexibility and an ability to adapt to differing practices. The offering is a practice that dates back to Old Testament times, linking money and personal finance directly to one's identity as a child of God. Giving of one's financial resources is an integral part of a healthy faith life.

**❶ Pay close attention to instructions, if any.**
The worship leader may announce the method of offering, or instructions may be printed in the worship bulletin or projected on an overhead screen.

**❷ Be alert for the plate's arrival at your row or pew.**
Keep an eye on the ushers, if there are any. In most churches, guiding and safeguarding the offering plate is the ushers' job, so wherever they are, so is the plate. As the plate approaches you, set aside other activity and prepare for passing.

**❸ Avoid watching your neighbor or making judgments about their offering.**
Many people contribute once a month by mail and some by automatic withdrawal from a bank account. If your neighbor passes the plate to you without placing an envelope, check, or cash in it, do not assume she or he didn't contribute.

**❹ Be discreet.**
Avoid being showy or obvious about your contribution. Give humbly.

**⑤** Place your offering in the plate as you pass it politely to the next person.

Do not attempt to make change from the plate if your offering is in cash. Avoid letting the plate rest in your lap as you finish writing a check. Simply pass it on and hand your check to an usher as you leave at the end of worship.

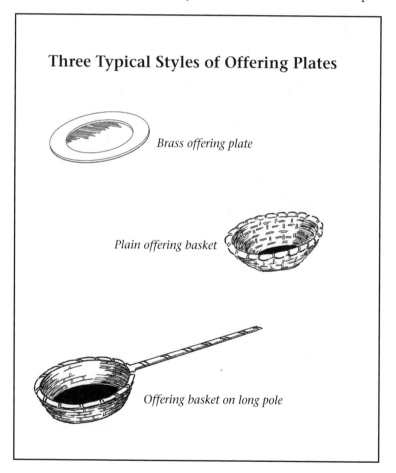

## Three Typical Styles of Offering Plates

*Brass offering plate*

*Plain offering basket*

*Offering basket on long pole*

⑥ Be sensitive to idiosyncrasies in plate types.
Some churches use traditional, wide-rimmed, felt-lined, brass-plated offering plates. Some use baskets of varying types. Some use cloth bags hung at the ends of long wooden poles that the ushers extend inward from the ends of the pews.

## Be Aware

- Some churches place the offering plate or basket at the rear of the worship space.

- Your church offering may be tax deductible, as provided by law. Consider making your offering by check or automatic withdrawal; you will receive a statement from your church in the first quarter of the next year.

- Churches often depend entirely upon the money that comes in through congregational offerings. If you are a member, resolve to work yourself toward tithing as a putting-your-money-where-your-mouth-is expression of faith. (The term *tithing* means "one-tenth" and refers to the practice of giving 10 percent of one's gross income to support God's work through the church.)

- Everyone, regardless of his or her age, has something to offer.

- Offerings are not fees or dues given out of obligation. They are gifts of thanksgiving returned to God from the heart.

# HOW TO GREET PEOPLE IN CHURCH

In Romans 16:16, Paul tells members of the congregation to "greet one another with a holy kiss." The First Letter of Peter ends: "Greet one another with a kiss of love. Peace to all of you who are in Christ" (1 Peter 5:14).

Some Christians worry about this part of the worship service due to its free-for-all nature. Some also feel uncomfortable because of their fear of being hugged. You can survive this, however, with these steps.

❶ **Adopt a peaceful frame of mind.**
Clear your mind of distracting and disrupting thoughts so you can participate joyfully and reverently.

❷ **Determine the appropriate form of safe touch.**
Handshaking is most common. Be prepared, however, for hugs, half-hugs, one-armed hugs, pats, and other forms of physical contact. Nods are appropriate for distances greater than two pews or rows.

❸ **Refrain from extraneous chitchat.**
This is not the time for lengthy introductions to new people, comments about the weather, or observations about yesterday's game. A brief encounter is appropriate, but save conversations for the coffee hour.

❹ **Make appropriate eye contact.**
Look the other person in the eye but do not stare. The action of looking the person in the eye highlights the relationship brothers and sisters in Christ have with one another.

*Make good eye contact as you greet others.*

**⑤ Greet the other person in Jesus' name.**
"Jesus loves you," "Peace be with you," "The peace of God," "God's peace," "The peace of Christ," and "Hello," are appropriate to say. Once spoken, move on to the next person.

## Be Aware

- Safe touch involves contact that occurs within your personal space but does not cause discomfort or unease.
- It is acceptable to state your first name and inquire as to the other person's first name.

# HOW TO STAY ALERT IN CHURCH

**❶ Get adequate sleep.**
Late Saturday nights are Sunday morning's worst enemy. Resolve to turn in earlier. A good night's sleep on Friday night is equally important to waking rested on Sunday, as sleep debt builds up over time.

**❷ Drink plenty of water, though not too much.**
It is easier to remain alert when you are well hydrated. Consider keeping a small bottle of water with you during worship. One quick bathroom break is considered permissible. Two or more are bad form.

**❸ Eat a high-protein breakfast.**
Foods high in carbohydrates force your body to metabolize them into sugars, which can make you drowsy. If your diet allows, eat foods high in protein instead, such as scrambled eggs with bacon.

**❹ Arrive early and find the coffee pot.**
If you don't drink coffee, consider a caffeinated soda.

**❺ Focus on your posture.**
Sit up straight with your feet planted firmly on the floor. Avoid slouching, as this encourages sleepiness. Good posture will promote an alert bearing and assist in paying attention, so you'll get more out of worship.

**❻ If you have difficulty focusing on the service, divert your attention. Occupy your mind, not your hands.**
Look around the worship space for visual stimuli. Keep your mind active in this way while continuing to listen.

**❼ Stay alert by flexing muscle groups in a pattern.**
Clench toes and feet; flex calf muscles, thighs, glutei,
abdomen, hands, arms, chest, and shoulders. Repeat.
Avoid shaking, rocking, or other movements that attract
undue attention.

**❽ If all else fails, consider pinching yourself.**
Dig your nails into the fleshy part of your arm or leg,
pinch yourself, bite down on your tongue with moderate
pressure. Try not to cry out.

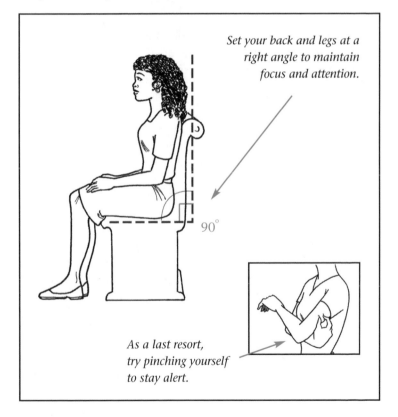

*Set your back and legs at a
right angle to maintain
focus and attention.*

90°

*As a last resort,
try pinching yourself
to stay alert.*

# WHAT TO BRING TO A CHURCH POTLUCK (BY REGION)

It is a generally followed practice in North American churches to enjoy three courses (commonly referred to as "dishes") at potlucks. Many of these dishes take on the flavor of the regions or cultures they represent. For best results, the preparer should understand the context in which the "dish" is presented.

## The Salad

Potluck salads are quite different from actual salads. In preparation for making a potluck salad, ask yourself three questions:

- Is this dish mostly meat-free?
- Can this dish be served with a spoon or salad tongs?
- Can it be served chilled?

If the answer is "yes" to any of these questions, consider the dish a potluck-eligible salad.

### The Mixture

This is the foundation of any potluck salad. It gives the salad a sense of direction. If at all possible, use ingredients that are indigenous to your area. For example, broccoli, lettuce, apples, macaroni, and candy bars are common in more temperate climates.

### The Crunchy Stuff

This component gives life and pizzazz to an otherwise bland salad. Examples: tortilla chips, shoestring potato crisps, onion crisps, and fried pigskins.

### The Glue

The glue holds the salad together. The variety of available types is stunning, ranging from a traditional oil-based salad dressing to mayonnaise and non-dairy whipped topping. Use your imagination. Consult regional recipes for exact ingredients.

*Note:* Some salads are best when made well in advance and allowed to sit overnight. This is called *marinating*, or "controlled decomposition." Do not use actual glue adhesive. Other salads are best prepared immediately before serving.

## The Casserole

A three-layered dish, typically. In order to make each casserole as culturally relevant as possible, use the following guidelines. Consult local restaurants for ideas, when in doubt.

### Starch

*East Coast:* pasta or rice pilaf

*Midwest:* rice, potatoes, noodles, or more rice

*South:* grits

*Southwest:* black, red, or pinto beans

*West Coast:* tofu

### Meat

*East Coast:* sausage or pheasant

*Midwest:* ground beef—in a pinch, SPAM® luncheon meat

*South:* crawdad or marlin

*Southwest:* pulled pork

*West Coast:* tofu

### Cereal

*East Coast:* corn flakes

*Midwest:* corn flakes

*South:* corn flakes

*Southwest:* corn flakes

*West Coast:* tofu flakes

*Note:* The starch and meat may be mixed with a cream-based soup. The cereal must always be placed on the top of the casserole.

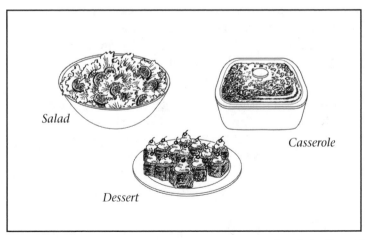

Salad

Casserole

Dessert

## The Dessert

The most highly valued dish at a potluck, this can be the simplest and most fun to make. There are two key ingredients:

1. flour
2. fudge

Regional influences can be quite profound. The following are examples of typical desserts around the country. Consult your church's seniors for the nuances of your region.

*Cleveland:* fudge brownies with fudge frosting

*Kansas City:* triple-fudge fudge with fudge sauce and a side of fudge

*Los Angeles:* tofu fudge

*Miami:* fudge

*New York City:* cheesecake with fudge drizzle

## Be Aware

- Use caution when preparing a dish. Adding local ingredients to any meat, salad, or dessert can increase the fellowship factor of your potluck exponentially. It also raises the risk of a "flop."

- Always follow safe food-handling guidelines.

- Any combination of flavored gelatin, shredded carrots, mini-marshmallows, and canned pears is an acceptable "utility" dish, should you be unable to prepare one from the above categories.

# HOW TO GET YOUR FAMILY TO CHURCH ON SUNDAY MORNING

Rounding up family members and moving them from home to pew requires different tools on different Sundays. Maintain flexibility in your struggle. Be proactive.

**❶ Shift into battle mode in advance of Saturday night.**
Obstacles may include Sunday morning cartoons, stubbornness, fatigue from Saturday evening activities, slow chewing at breakfast, and so on.

**❷ Approach the problem as a team whenever possible.**
In cases where two parents live in the household, both must support the decision to attend church regularly. Work it out together *prior* to Sunday morning. Remember, the family is not a democracy.

**❸ Make as many preparations as possible in advance of Sunday morning.**
Pre-select church clothes after checking the next day's forecast. Include matching dress socks and clean underwear. Plan a quick breakfast. Set multiple alarm clocks equipped with battery backup in case of power outages.

**❹ Preempt stomachaches, headaches, and other "illnesses."**
If a miraculous recovery following church appears imminent, make it clear that whatever illness and subsequent treatment comes for the morning, stays through the day.

**⑤ Make church an ironclad routine.**
"It's a church night," easily replaces, "It's a school night."

**⑥ Know the law: "Remember the sabbath day, and keep it holy."**
Relaxing, fishing, becoming one with nature, and washing the car do not count as keeping the sabbath. It's a Commandment; look it up.

**⑦ Pray for help. Miracles do happen.**

*Shift into Sunday morning mode on Saturday night.*

## Be Aware

- If your family reports disliking church, attempt to discover why and make changes when feasible. Be ready to adjust your own attitude to boost church-attendance morale among your family members.

- Both parents attending church is the single largest indicator of whether a child will attend church in adulthood. (According to a recent study, when both parents attend church regularly, 72 percent of children continue in the faith. When only the father attends, that percentage drops to 55 percent. But when only the mother attends, just 15 percent of children remain involved in the church.)

- People who attend worship are more likely to volunteer their time to make a positive contribution to society.

- How you spend your time is a reflection of your values and beliefs. Actions speak louder than words. Get driving.

- Consider bathing small children on Saturday night to save time Sunday morning.

# THE TOP FIVE CRITERIA FOR EVALUATING THE CHURCH NURSERY BEFORE PUTTING YOUR KIDS IN THERE

While some families choose to have their infants and toddlers accompany them to worship, the nursery is an important option for caregivers. Use the following criteria to assess a church nursery.

**❶ Overall nursery cleanliness.**
Make a cursory examination of the floors, walls, shelves, toys, play structures, and furniture. If it appears the nursery receives rare or inadequate cleaning, ask the pastor or person in charge of children's ministry for a copy of the schedule for vacuuming floors, cleaning walls and surfaces, and sanitizing toys.

**❷ Sturdy, sanitary diaper-changing station.**
This should be equipped with a safety belt to prevent the child from rolling off. Look for strategically placed anti-bacterial wipes or other cleaning products for sanitizing the changing surface after each use. Non-latex gloves should be provided.

**❸ Safe, clean toys.**
Some congregations accept all toy donations from members. While such generosity is well meant, this indiscriminate acceptance may lead to a sizable collection of broken, outdated, and unsafe toys. All toys should be in good condition and appropriate for all ages. Immediately report items that present a choking hazard. Goobers, boogers, crusties, and unidentifiable goo on toys should be thoroughly removed.

**4** Established or posted policies for nursery staff and volunteers.

A church nursery should have two or more leaders in the room at all times. Paid staff in particular should undergo background checks and have certification in infant and child CPR and first aid. Inquire about expectations for parents who volunteer and make sure that an adult is always present when youth serve as nursery helpers.

**5** Faith and fun.

A church nursery is an important context for faith formation of the church's youngest members. Toys, books, artwork, and staff attitudes should reflect a caring Christian environment. The nursery should also be a place where young children enjoy their time with nursery staff and other children.

## Be Aware

- In many congregations, when members offer ideas about improving facilities, they often find themselves leading a committee to make the changes.

- Don't hesitate to ask questions about policies and priorities when it comes to the care of your child and other children, Jesus' littlest followers.

*Goo of any kind should be removed from church nursery toys with a safe germicidal solution.*

# HOW TO PACK A DIAPER BAG FOR WORSHIP

Many families with infants and toddlers place their children in the nursery during worship. There is great value, however, in introducing a child to the worship life of a congregation. A well-stocked diaper bag will equip you to anticipate and defuse challenges that arise during a typical worship service.

**❶ Be prepared for impromptu feedings.**
Keep a bottle with formula or breast milk ready. If nursing, decide on a location before the service where you will feel comfortable feeding your baby. Consider packing a light blanket for privacy, if you prefer, but try not to alter your baby's feeding schedule. Burp cloths will protect your clothes from spit up and other messes.

**❷ Choose snacks wisely.**
Make sure your child's snacks are not too loud, crunchy, sticky, or crumbly. Toasted oat cereal and fish crackers are time-tested and tasty. Tidy up any crumbs or drooly tidbits.

**❸ Select a variety of quiet toys.**
Soft toys, such as stuffed animals, cloth finger puppets, and board books are all appropriate alternatives (especially if they are biblically themed) to playthings that make music or other sounds.

**❹ Include diapers, wipes, a changing pad, and an extra outfit.**
Savvy caregivers prepare for unexpected eliminations of all types. Stay alert for any leaks or unusual smells.

## Be Aware

- You are more likely to pack a well-stocked bag when you prepare it the night before worship. As with all things, think ahead.

- Research has shown that young children are more likely to show interest in items when they are new. Toys that a child sees only once a week are more interesting than toys he or she plays with every day.

- Many churches worship at several different times on a Sunday. Choose a worship time that corresponds well with your child's feeding and sleeping schedule.

- If you forget your diaper bag or find that you are missing key supplies, DO NOT PANIC. Most church nurseries stock extra diapers and wipes. Additionally, offering envelopes and attendance cards can substitute as toys and occupy children of many ages. Beware of paper cuts.

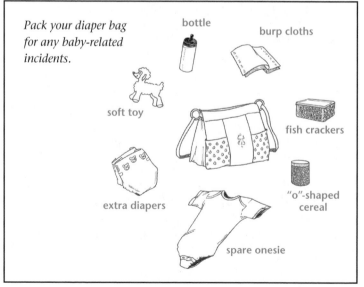

*Pack your diaper bag for any baby-related incidents.*

bottle

burp cloths

soft toy

fish crackers

extra diapers

"o"-shaped cereal

spare onesie

# HOW TO AVOID GETTING FED TO THE LIONS

Lions are fierce creatures and were used extensively as executioners throughout the ancient world. While getting fed to the lions is highly unlikely today, the Bible and early Christian history reveal several steps to avoid such a fate.

**1** **Pray three times a day, in a kneeling position, giving thanks to God regardless of your circumstances.** Daniel, an administrator to King Darius, continued to do this (Daniel 6:10) even when he learned Darius had issued a decree that anyone who prayed to a god or man other than the king himself would be thrown to the lions. Daniel was caught, placed in a lion's den, but found the next morning unharmed.

**2** **Beware of capricious, violent, and egomaniacal rulers.** In A.D. 64, the Roman emperor Nero falsely accused the Christians in Rome of setting a fire that consumed most of the city. As one of several cruel punishments, Nero fed many of these unfortunates to lions he had imported from Africa as entertainment in the coliseum. Hundreds of people were slaughtered in Nero's quest to stamp out the sect and elevate his own glory. Ironically, these executions further fanned the flames of the spreading the gospel of Jesus Christ and had the opposite effect of glorifying the Lord.

**3** **Consider making sacrifices to the hostile gods of any anti-Christian empires in which you might live.** Romans believed worship of the state gods was vital to preserve the empire's victory in war and prosperity at home.

Christians earmarked for death were given a chance by their "merciful" judges to renounce their beliefs, commonly by making a sacrifice to the health of the emperor or spreading incense over a lighted altar.

*Caution:* Christians who take their beliefs seriously will carefully consider the ramifications of making sacrifices to pagan gods—a direct violation of the First Commandment.

*In first-century Rome, lions posed a hazard above ground …*

*… to Christians, who often hid underground.*

**❹ Hide underground or "underground."**

The earliest Christian communities were driven to worship and even live in the city tombs, or catacombs, beneath the Roman streets. Because Nero and later Roman rulers hunted Christians with zeal, safety was better for Christians in the catacombs than for those who remained in the open. Those who lived above ground often lived double lives, practicing their faith in a secret and "underground" fashion.

*Outrunning a lion is probably not an option ...*

**❺ Escape.**

Escaping a lion on foot is impractical. At 50 miles per hour, lions run at double the speed of the fastest humans. A resourceful Christian (most likely acting in concert with other believers) can escape a lion feeding, however, by avoiding getting nabbed in the first place, or by fleeing to safety underground. Once set before a hungry lion, a human being has few prospects.

*... since lions run extremely fast.*

# COMPARATIVE RELIGIONS

| | Baha'i | Buddhism | Christianity |
|---|---|---|---|
| **Founder and date founded** | Bahá'u'lláh (1817-1892) founded Babism in 1844 from which Baha'i grew. | Founded by Siddhartha Gautama (the Buddha) in Nepal in the 6th-5th centuries B.C. | Founded by Jesus of Nazareth, a Palestinian Jew, in the early 1st century A.D. |
| **Number of adherents in 2000** | About 7 million worldwide; 750,000 U.S. | 360 million worldwide; 2 million U.S. | About 2 billion worldwide; 160 million U.S. |
| **Main tenets** | The oneness of God, the oneness of humanity, and the common foundation of all religion. Also, equality of men and women, universal education, world peace, and a world federal government. | Meditation and the practice of virtuous and moral behavior can lead to Nirvana, the state of enlightenment. Before that, one is subjected to repeated lifetimes, based on behavior. | Jesus is the Son of God and God in human form. In his death and resurrection, he redeems humanity from sin and gives believers eternal life. His teachings frame the godly life for his followers. |
| **Sacred or primary writing** | Bahá'u'lláh's teachings, along with those of the Bab, are collected and published. | The Buddha's teachings and wisdom are collected and published. | The Bible is a collection of Jewish and Near Eastern writings spanning some 1,400 years. |

| Confucianism | Hinduism | Islam | Judaism |
|---|---|---|---|
| Founded by the Chinese philosopher Confucius in the 6th-5th centuries B.C. One of several traditional Chinese religions. | Developed in the 2nd century B.C. from indigenous religions in India, and later combined with other religions, such as Vaishnavism. | Founded by the prophet Muhammad ca. A.D. 610. The word *Islam* is Arabic for "submission to God." | Founded by Abraham, Isaac, and Jacob ca. 2000 B.C. |
| 6 million worldwide (does not include other traditional Chinese beliefs); U.S. uncertain. | 900 million worldwide; 950,000 U.S. | 1.3 billion worldwide; 5.6 million U.S. | 14 million worldwide; 5.5 million U.S. |
| Confucius's followers wrote down his sayings or *Analects*. They stress relationships between individuals, families, and society based on proper behavior and sympathy. | Hinduism is based on a broad system of sects. The goal is release from repeated reincarnation through yoga, adherence to the Vedic scriptures, and devotion to a personal guru. | Followers worship Allah through the Five Pillars. Muslims who die believing in God, and that Muhammad is God's messenger, will enter Paradise. | Judaism holds the belief in a monotheistic God, whose Word is revealed in the Hebrew Bible, especially the Torah. Jews await the coming of a messiah to restore creation. |
| Confucius's *Analects* are collected and still published. | The Hindu scriptures and Vedic texts. | The Koran is a collection of Muhammad's writings. | The Hebrew scriptures compose the Christian Old Testament. |

# COMPARATIVE DENOMINATIONS

| | Adventist | Anabaptist | Anglican |
|---|---|---|---|
| **Founded when and by whom?** | 1844: William Miller's prediction of Christ's return that year failed. 1863: Seventh-Day Adventist Church is organized. | 1523: Protestants in Zurich, Switzerland, begin believers' baptism. 1537: Menno Simons begins Mennonite movement. | 1534: Henry VIII is declared head of the Church of England. 1549: Thomas Cranmer produces the first *Book of Common Prayer*. |
| **Adherents in 2000?** | About 11 million worldwide; about 100,000 U.S. | About 2 million worldwide; about 600,000 U.S. | 45-75 million worldwide; about 3 million U.S. |
| **How is Scripture viewed?** | Protestant canon accepted. Scripture is inspired and without error; Ellen G. White, an early leader, was a prophet. | Protestant canon accepted. Scripture is inspired but not infallible. Jesus is living Word; Scripture is written Word. | Protestant canon accepted. Scripture is interpreted in light of tradition and reason. |
| **How are we saved?** | We repent by believing in Christ as Example (in his life) and Substitute (by his death). Those who are found right with God will be saved. | Salvation is a personal experience. Through faith in Jesus, we become at peace with God, moving us to follow Jesus' example by being peacemakers. | We share in Christ's victory, who died for our sins, freeing us through baptism to become living members of the church. |
| **What is the church?** | Includes all who believe in Christ. The last days are a time of apostasy, when a remnant keeps God's commandments faithfully. | The body of Christ, the assembly and society of believers. No one system of government is recognized. | The body of Christ is based on "apostolic succession" of bishops, going back to the apostles. In the U.S., it is the Episcopal Church. |
| **What about the sacraments?** | Baptism is the immersion of believers only. Baptism and the Lord's Supper are symbolic only. | Baptism is for believers only. The Lord's Supper is a memorial of his death. | Baptism brings infant and convert initiates into the church; in Communion, Christ's body & blood are truly present. |

|  | **Baptist** | **Catholic** | **Churches of Christ** |
|---|---|---|---|
| **Founded when and by whom?** | 1612: John Smythe and other Puritans form the first Baptist church. 1639: The first Baptist church in America is established. | Catholics consider Jesus' disciple Peter (died ca. A.D. 66) the first pope. Through Gregory the Great (540-604), papacy is firmly established. | 1801: Barton Stone holds Cane Ridge Revival in Kentucky. 1832: Stone's Christians unite with Disciples of Christ. |
| **Adherents in 2000?** | 100 million worldwide; about 30 million U.S. | About 1 billion worldwide; 60 million U.S. | 5-6 million worldwide; about 3 million U.S. |
| **How is Scripture viewed?** | Protestant canon accepted. Scripture is inspired and without error; the sole rule of faith. | The canon is 46 books in the OT (Apocryhpha included) and 27 in the NT. Interpretation is subject to church tradition. | Protestant canon accepted. Scripture is the Word of God. Disciples of Christ view it as a witness to Christ, but fallible. |
| **How are we saved?** | Salvation is offered freely to all who accept Jesus as Savior. There is no salvation apart from personal faith in Christ. | God infuses the gift of faith in the baptized, which is maintained by good works and receiving Penance and the Eucharist. | We must hear the gospel, repent, confess Christ, and be baptized. Disciples of Christ: God saves people by grace. |
| **What is the church?** | The body of Christ; the redeemed throughout history. The term *church* usually refers to local congregations, which are autonomous. | The mystical body of Christ, who established it with the pope as its head; he pronounces doctrine infallibly. | The assembly of those who have responded rightly to the gospel; it must be called only by the name of Christ. |
| **What about the sacraments?** | Baptism is immersion of believers, only as a symbol. The Lord's Supper is symbolic. | Catholics hold seven sacraments. Baptism removes original sin; usually infants. The Eucharist undergoes transubstantiation. | Baptism is the immersion of believers only, as the initial act of obedience to the gospel. The Lord's Supper is a symbolic memorial. |

# COMPARATIVE DENOMINATIONS

| | Congregational | Lutheran | Methodist |
|---|---|---|---|
| **Founded when and by whom?** | 1607: Members of England's illegal "house church" exiled. 1620: Congregationalists arrive in the New World on the *Mayflower*. | 1517: Martin Luther challenges Catholic teachings with his Ninety-five Theses. 1530: the Augsburg Confession is published. | 1738: Anglican ministers John and Charles Wesley convert. 1784: U.S. Methodists form a separate church body. |
| **Adherents in 2000?** | More than 2 million worldwide; about 2 million U.S. | About 60 million worldwide; about 9 million U.S. | 20-40 million worldwide; about 13 million U.S. |
| **How is Scripture viewed?** | Protestant canon accepted. Bible is the authoritative witness to the Word of God. | Protestant canon contains 39 OT books, 27 NT. Scripture alone is the authoritative witness to the gospel. | Protestant canon accepted. Scripture is primary source for Christian doctrine. |
| **How are we saved?** | God promises forgiveness and grace to save "from sin and aimlessness" all who trust him, who accept his call to serve the whole human family. | We are saved by grace when God grants righteousness through faith alone. Good works inevitably result, but they are not the basis of salvation. | We are saved by grace alone. Good works must result, but do not obtain salvation. |
| **What is the church?** | The people of God living as Jesus' disciples. Each local church is self-governing and chooses its own ministers. | The congregation of believers, mixed with the lost, in which the gospel is preached and the sacraments are administered. | The body of Christ, represented by church institutions. Bishops oversee regions and appoint pastors, who are itinerant. |
| **What about the sacraments?** | Congregations may practice infant baptism or believers' baptism or both. Sacraments are symbols. | Baptism is necessary for salvation. The Lord's Supper is bread & wine that, with God's Word are truly Jesus' body & blood. | Baptism is a sign of regeneration; in the Lord's Supper, Jesus is really present. |

|  | Orthodox | Pentecostal | Presbyterian |
|---|---|---|---|
| **Founded when and by whom?** | A.D 330: Emperor Constantine renames Byzantium "Constantinople" and declares Christianity the empire's religion. | 1901: Kansas college students speak in tongues. 1906: Azusa Street revival in L.A. launches movement. 1914: Assemblies of God organized. | 1536: John Calvin writes *Institutes of the Christian Religion*. 1789: Presbyterian Church U.S.A. is organized. |
| **Adherents in 2000?** | About 225 million worldwide; about 4 million U.S. | About 500 million worldwide; about 5 million U.S. | 40-48 million worldwide; 4 million U.S. |
| **How is Scripture viewed?** | 49 OT books (Catholic plus three more) and 27 NT. Scripture is subject to tradition. | Protestant canon accepted. Scripture is inspired and without error. Some leaders are considered prophets. | Protestant canon accepted. Scripture is "witness without parallel" to Christ, but in human words reflecting beliefs of the time. |
| **How are we saved?** | God became human so humans could be deified, that is, have the energy of God's life in them. | We are saved by God's grace through Jesus, resulting in our being born again in the Spirit, as evidenced by a life of holiness. | We are saved by grace alone. Good works result, but are not the basis of salvation. |
| **What is the church?** | The body of Christ in unbroken historical connection with the apostles; the Roman pope is one of many patriarchs who govern. | The body of Christ, in which the Holy Spirit dwells; the agency for bringing the gospel of salvation to the whole world. | The body of Christ includes all of God's chosen and is represented by the visible church. Governed by regional "presbyteries" of elders. |
| **What about the sacraments?** | Baptism initiates God's life in the baptized; adults and children. In the Eucharist, bread & wine are changed into body & blood. | Baptism is immersion of believers only. A further "baptism in the Holy Spirit" is offered. Lord's Supper is symbolic. | Baptism is not necessary for salvation. The Lord's Supper is Christ's body & blood, which are spiritually present to believers. |

# PARTS OF A CHURCH BUILDING —TRADITIONAL

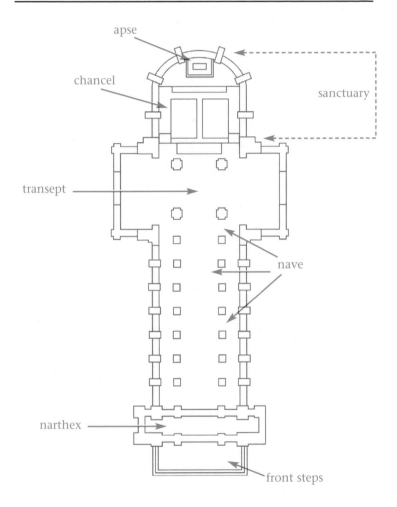

apse

chancel

sanctuary

transept

nave

narthex

front steps

# PARTS OF A CHURCH BUILDING —MODERN

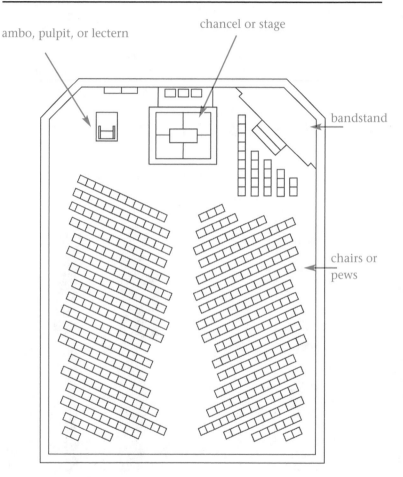

ambo, pulpit, or lectern

chancel or stage

bandstand

chairs or pews

*Note:* In modern churches, the entire worship space is often called the "sanctuary."

# COMMON TYPES OF CLERGY GARB

Clergy in different traditions wear different clothing in their work. Each serves a particular function.

*In some traditions, clergy emphasize the academic side of pastoring and interpreting the Bible, often wearing academic-style robes.*

*The alb and stole represent the Holy Spirit's presence and the yoke of Christ.*

academic robe
with chevrons

stole

alb

*In some traditions, a clergyperson of higher authority, such as a bishop, may wear a miter. The chasuble typically is worn for celebrating the Eucharist.*

*To signify their role among their congregants and the universal nature of Christian ministry, some clergy dress in sharp suits.*

miter

chasuble

sharp suit

# *EVERYDAY STUFF*

Believing in God involves more than going to church and reading the Bible. It's about keeping your faith with you in every part of your life.

This section includes:

- Advice for helping people in times of trouble.
- Tips on forgiving others and treating them with respect—even if you don't always feel like it.
- Suggestions for avoiding temptation on a daily basis.

# HOW TO LISTEN FOR GOD'S VOICE

Listening for God's voice is an essential skill throughout the range of the Christian experience, but different experiences demand slightly different listening skills.

## Times of Woe

Woe is a common human experience, and it is natural to wonder what you did to deserve it. But during a time of woe, even amid the pain, there is an accompanying openness of spirit God can use.

**❶ Don't be afraid to question God.**

You'll be in good company. Job asked questions. Moses asked questions. Even Jesus asked questions. God can handle your most passionate questions. In fact, God welcomes them. This kind of honest prayer is exactly what God wants from people.

**❷ Spend time reading God's Word.**

God uses the Holy Scriptures to enlighten minds, clarify thinking, and comfort persons enduring times of woe. Occasionally the effect may be understood more on an emotional level than on a rational level. Consider crying out for God's comfort. Psalms are particularly helpful in this case.

**❸ Seek out brothers and sisters in Christ.**

Sharing sorrow with the family of God, though sometimes painful, can significantly mitigate woe. Remain open to the possibility that the words of other people might reflect the very things God is saying to you during this time—but realize that even well-meaning people might say silly and even unhelpful things as well.

*God's Word provides great comfort during times of woe.*

**❹** Keep listening.

You may hear nothing specific from God immediately, but the Bible says every circumstance of life can be an opportunity for God's purposes to move forward. An ear open to God bespeaks a heart open to God.

## Times of Joy

While times of joy are typically considered less instructional than times of woe, an ear open to God's voice can nonetheless yield great wisdom. Do not allow this to impede your celebrations, however.

**❶** Rejoice.

The thankful attitude of a joyful Christian is like a fragrant flower garden to God. Nearby persons will likely respond with joy, too. God often answers thankfulness with even more to be grateful for.

*Rejoice shamelessly when God provides a time of joy. Consider skipping when possible.*

**❷ Share the joy and the message.**
Your buoyant spirit can lift others. Don't overwhelm people, but do share. Avoid becoming preachy, overbearing, insensitive, or running roughshod over woeful persons.

**❸ Spend time reading God's Word, especially passages in which the author rejoices.**
Placing your joy in the context of biblical joy can frame your experience and increase your joy as well as your ability to listen for God's voice.

**❹ Skip down your block unashamedly and let people talk.**
The gospel often inspires reckless disregard for stifling social norms. Allowing yourself to indulge these impulses —within reason—can further open your heart to God's messages and make you an unrestrained evangelist for Jesus Christ.

## Every Day

**1** Develop a routine of listening. Practice the discipline of keeping your mouth closed, except when eating and answering questions.

Consider turning off the radio while driving so you can listen for God's voice, or rising early in the morning to read a portion of the Bible and pray. Suppress the urge to interrupt others in conversation.

**2** Remember God moment by moment.

Once you overcome the need for constant verbal expression and the craving to fill your senses with artificial noise and stimulation, you can begin truly listening for the still, small voice of God in every moment of the day.

**3** Look for opportunities to remember God aloud to others.

God has put a desire to know him in every human being. When the Holy Spirit opens the opportunity, speaking the gospel to others can, in itself, facilitate God's voice in the world and make you a co-creator with him.

# HOW TO COMMIT YOUR WAY TO THE LORD

There is a path many Christians walk that helps them give over their plans and desires to God and find peace rather than worry. This path involves a union of their desires with the desires of their King, who would ultimately be in charge of the direction and outcome of their lives.

This is also the path of which King David said, "Commit your way to the LORD; trust in him and he will do this" (Psalm 37:5). When you find yourself worrying over your plans instead of enjoying peace, follow the steps below.

**❶ Enter into prayer. Outline your goal, go through the specifics, and bring all aspects of your goal clearly into view.**
Do this in frank conversation with God, allowing him to hear your plans and desires and dreams. Discuss these goals and plans with him openly and honestly.

**❷ Keep an open heart and mind.**
God's plans may be different from yours. Once you've told God clearly what you want and examined that desire in light of the priorities of God's Word, release that desire to him without reservation.

**❸ Observe. Watch carefully what God does. Expect surprises.**
Every day is an adventure when you commit your way to the Lord. God directs your paths, opens doors, makes a way for you where there was no way, and closes doors at times so you'll walk a different way.

**❹ Obey God and proceed with trust.**

Your way is now committed to the Lord. When he wants to accomplish something, heaven and earth cannot prevail against him.

## Be Aware

- The devil takes notice when you commit your way to God and will likely seek to derail you. Fear not. God has got hold of you.

- The more tightly you cling to your own plans, the more difficult it will be to release them to God.

*To commit your way to the Lord, begin with prayer.*

# HOW TO SHARE YOUR FAITH WITH SOMEONE

Sharing the gospel with others is a natural part of exercising a mature faith. In fact, Jesus commanded his followers to do this, making it an important part of the life of faith (Matthew 28:18-20). Still, some Christians tend to be rather shy evangelists. While *evangelism* has become a negative word for some people, sharing the story of salvation in Jesus Christ is still the most rewarding way to live out one's faith. It is also a discipline that takes practice.

**❶ Look for the opening.**
Regular daily conversations offer lots of chances to talk about your faith. Listen for open-ended comments, such as, "I wonder why life is like that," or, "Sometimes life seems so hard." When possible, offer a response from a Christian perspective. Begin sentences with phrases such as, "I've come to think ...," or, "I don't have the perfect answer, but I believe ..."

**❷ Be yourself.**
Expressing your faith should be natural and the same as other types of daily conversation. Avoid suddenly switching your tone of voice or vocabulary. Also, don't try to impress the other person with your knowledge. Allow the Holy Spirit to guide you.

**❸ Watch for a chance to take the conversation deeper.**
Carefully gauge the other person's response. Observe his or her facial expression, verbal tone, and body language. If he or she seems to be closing down, set the topic aside and wait for another time. If he or she keys in and perks up, be prepared to continue.

**4** Open up.

Human beings are attracted to each other by our strengths, but we bond because of our weaknesses. Key to sharing your faith is the willingness to be honest about your own life's struggles. This will communicate safety, which for many people is critical.

**5** Follow up.

Offer to continue the conversation later and arrange a time. At this point, the conversation will have become personally valuable to you. Allowing the person to see your commitment to your faith alongside your continuing questions will reassure him or her of your sincerity.

**6** Offer to share your faith community with the other person.

Most people join a church after being invited by a friend. When the time is right, invite the person to attend with you. Tell the person what makes it special to you.

**7** Try to maintain the relationship regardless of what the person does.

Be prepared for the other person to shut down around faith talk, decline your invitation to attend church, or even appear to avoid you. The most effective way to communicate that you're a follower of Jesus Christ is through your actions; continue to live naturally and with integrity. Watch for another opportunity to open the subject later on.

# HOW TO PRAY

Prayer is intimate communication with God and can be used before a meal, at bedtime, during a church service, or any time the need or opportunity arises. Silent and spoken prayers are both okay and may be used liberally throughout the day. Prayer is also taking time to listen to what God is saying to us. Spontaneous prayer is often best, but the following process may help build the habit.

❶ Assess your need for prayer.
Take stock of the situation at hand, including your motivations. What are you praying *for* and why?

❷ Consider selecting a type of prayer.
Prayers of *supplication* (requests for God's help), *contrition* (in which sin is confessed and forgiveness requested), *intercession* (on behalf of others), and others are good and time tested. Books of personal prayers, hymnals, and devotionals often contain helpful, prewritten prayers. Consider also an ad-libbed prayer from the heart.

❸ Select a physical prayer posture.
Many postures are appropriate:

- The most common type of prayer in the New Testament is from a prone position, lying face-down on the ground, arms spread.

- Kneeling with your face and palms upturned is good for prayers of supplication.

- Bowed head with closed eyes and hands folded is common today and aids concentration.

There is no "official" posture for prayer. Choose your posture according to your individual prayer needs.

*Choose a comfortable and appropriate prayer posture for your prayer time.*

**❹ Offer your prayer.**
Pray with confidence. God listens to all prayer and responds. Breathe deeply, relax, and be open as the Spirit leads you.

**❺ Listen.**
Take time during your prayer simply to listen. Some prayer traditions involve only silent meditation as a means of listening for God's voice.

## Be Aware

- God hears every prayer.
- Prayer can be done either alone or in the company of others (corporately).
- Environment matters. If possible, consider lighting a candle and dimming the lights to set the correct mood and help block out distractions.

# HOW TO DO GOOD ON BEHALF OF PEOPLE WHO ARE POOR AND OPPRESSED

Christian churches around the globe traditionally set this as one of their highest priorities, giving time, labor, and money both locally and globally to those who are less fortunate. As a follower of Jesus Christ, each individual Christian is linked to Jesus' compassion for people who are poor and called to work tirelessly on their behalf, as he did.

**❶ Include people who are poor and oppressed in your daily prayers.**

Keeping the needs of others in mind, especially people who suffer as a result of economic inequality, political oppression, or natural disaster, defines a person's good works. Name specific situations in your prayers, and use specific place names and people's names whenever possible. Keep the newspaper on your lap as you pray, if necessary.

**❷ Include people who are poor and oppressed in your personal or household budget.**

Dedicate some of your personal giving to economic-aid organizations. This should include your congregation. If you already tithe (give 10 percent of your income to your church), consider earmarking a percentage of that money to go directly to relief organizations through your church's budget.

**❸** Pay close attention to economic and political conditions in other nations.

You can't help if you don't know what's really going on. Resolve to be a well-informed person who tests the worldview in the news against the worldview in the Bible.

**❹** Get to know organizations that work for justice locally.

Your congregation probably already organizes to do justice work in your neighborhood. If not, consider taking responsibility to organize a ministry team in your church.

**❺** Make working for justice part of your weekly or monthly routine.

Devote a portion of your time regularly to a specific activity that personally connects you to people who are poor and disenfranchised. There is no substitute for personal contact.

**❻** Vote your conscience.

If you are of voting age, remember that nations will be judged by the way they treat people who are disadvantaged. Keep this in mind when you go to your polling place.

**❼** Advocate for a cause in which you believe, one that has meaning for you personally.

# HOW TO IDENTIFY A GENUINE MIRACLE

The term *miracle* describes something that causes wonder. It is usually used in reference to an event that defies logical explanation and appears to be the work of a higher force, suggesting a reality beyond the five senses.

**❶ Disregard most minor situations.**

The facts should indicate a situation of high order, such as one that is life threatening, one involving suffering, or involving an immediate threat. Finding your lost keys does not necessarily constitute a miracle.

**❷ Look for a lack of predictability.**

A positive outcome should be needed and wanted, but not expected. Miracles tend to occur out of the blue rather than as the result of an earthly cause, especially a human one.

**❸ Evaluate the outcome.**

Miracles achieve a life-giving purpose; they never occur outside the will of God. Suffering is relieved, God is glorified, Jesus' presence is made manifest, the lowly are lifted up, evil is thwarted, creation is revealed, or life is saved. The outcome *must* be regarded as good, according to biblical standards.

**❹ Look for a divine agency.**

The ability to make a miracle happen, to guarantee the results, or to take credit for it is beyond human. Often, the event will defy what we know to be true about the laws of nature or probability. If anyone stands to make money or advance an agenda from an event, it is most likely not a miracle.

**⑤** Adopt a wait-and-see perspective.

A miracle will still be a miracle later on. Labeling something a miracle too quickly could lead down unhelpful paths, while waiting to make the call—pondering the event in your heart—will enhance your faith journey.

## Be Aware

- The most overlooked miracle is that God shows up in everyday life events.

- The miracle of life in Jesus Christ is a daily event and should be regarded as a free gift.

*Finding a lost set of keys probably doesn't constitute a miracle.*

# THE ANATOMY OF A GOOD WORK

God is the one who motivates and completes all good works.

Hearts are comforted and strengthened through good works (2 Thessalonians 2:17).

God intends for good works to meet people's needs (Titus 3:14).

Good works are often public acts in the name of Jesus (1 Timothy 5:25).

It's good to do certain good works in public (Matthew 5:16), but *not* for your own glory.

Good works do not bring salvation (Ephesians 2:8-9) but rather are the Christian way of life.

All persons were created for good works (Ephesians 2:10). In this case, the woman crosses the street safely and the Boy Scout fulfills his duty.

# HOW TO AVOID POLLYANNAISM

Identifying Pollyannaism is relatively easy: it is marked by an over-the-top, syrupy happiness that excludes all other emotions and states of mind. A more balanced and reality-based approach to life is the hallmark of Christianity and the basis of a healthy faith.

A person who practices Pollyannaism is called a "Pollyanna" and may be identified by an inclination to cloak real problems with a Christian garment by saying everything is "okay" or "wonderful" when in fact it is not. Life includes real pain, real trouble, and real sorrow, and Christians are honest about it. To deny this or to act as if such things do not affect you is to bend credibility with others, with God, and with yourself.

## Signs of Being a Pollyanna

❶ Pollyannas often spontaneously break into song with "Climb, Climb Up Sunshine Mountain." Hardcore Pollyannas perform the accompanying hand actions. They may look you in the eye and nod, hoping you will join in as well. *Caution:* Do not, under any circumstances, attempt the motions to "Climb, Climb Up Sunshine Mountain," as permanent damage to your irony organ may result.

❷ Pollyannas cut off honest talk of any kind, seeking instead a train of thought that lifts them into unrealistic optimism and happiness. Be careful not to board that train yourself.

❸ When asked, "How are you?" even in passing, Pollyannas often respond by gushing, "Blessed!"

## Steps to Avoid Pollyannaism

**❶ Establish a habit of honesty regarding trouble or problems.**
Christians are perfectly free in Jesus Christ by virtue of faith in him, and therefore need not fear the truth about anything, even themselves. Approach problems with this fact in mind.

**❷ Embrace the potential for a positive outcome, regardless of present circumstances, but do not fixate on it.**
Recognize that God wants to provide something new and positive for you in the middle of the trouble, which can only be discovered by facing it.

**❸ Depend on God in prayer.**
In the safety of prayer, all truth can be faced, no matter how difficult. Once faced, it can be overcome.

Pollyanna

Regular Christian on a good day.

**④ Avoid wishing that a trouble would go away.**
This is not the same as a trouble actually going away.
It is only wishing.

**⑤ Where appropriate, speak openly with others about the pain and suffering you experience.**
It is important that others know you struggle. In fact, you can actually encourage a brother or sister by telling about your own struggles, but avoid overburdening your listener with too much detail. Allow them to draw you into conversation.

**⑥ Gently taboo Pollyannaism when you encounter it.**
Poking good-natured (not mean-spirited) fun at Pollyannaism can be a healthy reminder of the honesty that is a critical part of Christian life and can help retrieve a Pollyanna from wrong-headedness.

## Be Aware

- Pollyannaism is not a terminal condition. Many Christians have recovered from apparently debilitating cases of Pollyannaism to become balanced, well-adjusted people.

- Beware over-compensating for a perceived case of Pollyannaism by becoming bitter or constantly negative. Faith in Christ often brings joy.

# THREE ESSENTIAL PERSONAL SPIRITUAL RITUALS

A spiritual ritual is a routine for building one's faith. Ritual involves action, words, and often images that work together to center one's daily life in Jesus Christ. Medical studies show that people who pray regularly throughout the day suffer less stress, have lower incidence of heart disease, and live longer on average than those who do not.

**❶ Morning devotions.**

- Directly upon awakening, turn your attention first to God. The silence and solitude available in the morning hours are ideal.

- Try to make prayer the first activity of your day. If necessary, set your alarm to sound 15 minutes early to give yourself time.

- Begin with thanks and by remembering God's constant presence in Jesus.

- Identify events you anticipate in your day and how you feel about them.

- Ask God to provide what you need for the day.

- Pray on behalf of other people. Consider keeping a list of names tucked inside your Bible or devotional book.

**❷** Mealtime grace.

Human beings naturally pause before a meal. Use those moments to give thanks.

- Consider establishing mealtime grace as a household ritual.

- When eating in public, be considerate of others, but do not abandon your ritual.

- Once your meal is assembled and ready to eat, take time before praying to gather your thoughts and call an appropriate prayer to mind.

- Many people pray a rote or memorized prayer at mealtimes. Consider occasionally departing from your regular prayer with an extemporaneous one.

*Praying before mealtime is a great personal ritual that can be shared with others.*

**❸** Evening prayer.

The other daily rituals you perform in the evening, like brushing your teeth or letting the cat out, create a natural structure for evening prayer.

- Establish a regular time, such as sunset or at bedtime, and commit to it.

- Confess sins and ask for forgiveness.

- Tell God about the joys and sorrows of the day. Ask for help with the sorrows and give thanks for the joys.

- Identify the good things about the day. On bad days, find at least one thing to give thanks for.

- Consider using a devotional as a guide and companion.

- Think about involving other members of your household in this ritual. Evening prayer particularly can be enhanced through sharing.

- Spouses may find evening prayer to be the most comfortable time for their devotions together.

# HOW TO REPENT

Christians regard repentance as a fundamental benefit of the Christian life. Jesus said, "The kingdom of God is near. Repent and believe the good news" (Mark 1:15). The New Testament word for *repent* means "to change one's mind," as in to change one's heart and life completely. The Old Testament word for *repent* means "to turn," as in to turn away from sin and back to God.

Repentance is about turning away from sin and turning back toward God. God calls us to repent both "once" in our lives and also "every day." Those who don't know the Lord repent "once"—to turn toward the Lord and be saved by God's grace. Those who already know the Lord repent "every day"—to turn away from the evil and sin that tempts us, and turn back to God. In both cases, the method of repentance is the same.

**❶ Hear God's Word.**
God's Word instructs us about the sin in our lives. The Word shows us those things about us that are not of God. God's Word comes to us through Jesus, through the Scriptures, and through preaching.

**❷ Recognize and admit your sin.**
Part of repentance is acknowledging our sin and being sorry for the wrong we do: "Godly sorrow brings repentance" (2 Corinthians 7:10). Tell God you know you sin and that you are sorry for your sin.

**❸ Ask the Holy Spirit for help turning back to God.**
A person cannot repent or turn to God on his or her own. Ask God for help. Pray in the name of Jesus that the Holy Spirit would come to you and turn you back to the Lord.

**❹ Live as a forgiven sinner.**
God wants us to live in the way that is best for us and best for our neighbors—a way that points to God. Live according to God's will, loving God and your neighbor with all your heart.

**❺ Repeat the process daily.**
Repentance is a way of life. Every day brings new opportunities to hear God's Word, acknowledge and be sorry for the wrong we do, ask God for help, and live as forgiven sinners.

## Be Aware

- In cases when no particular sin can be called to mind, repentance should nonetheless be undertaken earnestly. Simply tell God that you are sorry for sins you are not aware of. You have certainly committed some.

# HOW TO FORGIVE SOMEONE

Forgiving is one of the most difficult disciplines of faith, since it seems to cost you something additional when you've already been wronged. Swallowing your pride and seeking a greater good, however, can yield great healing and growth.

**1 Acknowledge that God forgives you.**
When you realize that God has already shown forgiveness, and continues to forgive sinners like you, it's easier to forgive someone else.

**2 Consult Scripture.**
Jesus taught the Lord's Prayer to his disciples, who were hungry to become like he was. Forgiveness was a big part of this. Read Matthew 6:9-15.

**3 Seek the person out whenever possible.**
Consciously decide to deliver your forgiveness in person. In cases where this is geographically impossible, find an appropriate alternative means, such as the telephone.

*Note:* This may not be wise in all cases, given the timing of the situation or the level of hurt. Certain problems can be made worse by an unwelcome declaration of forgiveness. Consult with a clergyperson before taking questionable action.

**4 Say, "I forgive you," out loud.**
A verbal declaration of forgiveness is ideal. Speaking the words enacts a physical chain reaction that can create healing for both speaker and hearer. In the Bible, Jesus used these words to heal a paralyzed man from across a room.

**❺** Pray for the power to forgive.

Praying for this is always good, whether a forgiveness situation is at hand or not. It is especially helpful in cases where declaring forgiveness seems beyond your reach.

## Be Aware

- When someone sins against you personally, forgiving them does NOT depend upon them feeling sorry (showing contrition) or asking for your forgiveness. But it helps. You may have to struggle, however, to forgive them without their consent or participation.

# How to Tell a Sinner from a Saint

Sinner       Saint

*It's impossible to tell a sinner from a saint, because all people are fully both. Churches are filled with them.*

# HOW TO CONFESS YOUR SINS AND RECEIVE FORGIVENESS

**1** Make a mental list of your offenses.

**2** Locate a fellow Christian.
When appropriate, confess your sins to another person.

**3** Resolve to confess of your own free will.
Don't confess merely because someone else wants you to do it. Make your confession voluntarily.

**4** Make your confession fearlessly, aloud if possible.
Confess the sins that burden you, and then confess the sins of which you are not aware or can't remember.

**5** Avoid making up sins.
More important than the facts and figures is a spirit of repentance in your heart.

**6** Receive forgiveness with a believing heart.
God forgives you fully. Believe it. Consider making the sign of the cross or praying a brief prayer to help you remember.

**7** Resolve to live joyfully.
With forgiveness comes new life in the freedom of God's grace.

## Be Aware

- Unburdening your conscience through the confession of sins is cleansing and good for the soul; it's not meant to be torture.

- Ultimately, forgiveness comes from God. A perfect confession of sins is not a strict requirement to receive it.

# HOW TO DEFEND YOUR FAITH AGAINST ATTACK

Defending your faith from attack involves tact and savvy, that is, the ability to empathize with your adversary and use his or her affronts creatively without getting baited into an angry or hostile response. Just be ready. There is no substitute for knowing your stuff.

**1 Employ the 80/20 rule.**
In any debate, it is best to listen at least 80 percent of the time and talk 20 percent of the time.

**2 Engage in empathic listening.**
Empathic listening means to try to comprehend not just the content of the other person's position, but also the emotional thrust behind it. This is important especially in cases where the speaker's emotional expressions are intense.

**3 Restate your adversary's argument empathetically.**
Use sentences like, "So, you're upset because Christians seem to say one thing and do another."

**4 Identify with what the speaker is saying.**
For example, say, "I know what you mean. I see a lot of phony behavior at my own church." This elevates the conversation and keeps it civil.

**5 Do your best to put the speaker at ease.**
Having made clear that you understand his or her position, you are free to state your defense or counter-point. Offer "I statement" responses, such as, "I wonder how I would stand up under that kind of scrutiny, myself," or, "I do my best not to judge others too harshly. I'd hate to be judged by those standards."

**6** Keep it as upbeat as possible.
Use humility, humor, and a pleasant nature to defuse any tension. Though hard to practice, it is possible to disagree with someone while remaining friends.

**7** Give your opponent his or her due.
When the speaker makes a good argument, say, "You make a good point." This will further elevate the conversation. If you still disagree, make your counter-argument calmly.

**8** Avoid closing off the conversation or leaving it on a sour note.
If you can, offer to continue the discussion over a lunch that you buy. Avoid falling into a "winner take all" mind-set. Keep respect as your highest value.

## Be Aware

- Attacks on faith are not limited to verbal assaults, especially in countries such as China or Vietnam, where religious persecution is a reality. Take care when visiting such places, especially when distributing religious materials or sharing stories about your faith.

- It is best in all cases to avoid sounding smug or preachy where your points resemble counterattacks.

# HOW TO RESIST TEMPTATION

Asserting faith in Christ naturally places people at odds with certain activities and beliefs. It also draws the attention of the Tempter, who aims to confuse believers and separate them from God. Temptation is the constant companion of a Christian, but its effects can be mitigated and often overcome.

**❶ Run the opposite direction.**
Learn to identify the things that tempt you and avoid situations in which temptation will occur. When you see a temptation coming down the road, take a detour.

**❷ Laugh at the Tempter.**
Temptations are simply things that want to gain power over you. When you laugh at them, you reduce them to their proper place.

**❸ Distract yourself with other, healthier activities.**
God knows what's good for you and so do you. Find an alternate activity that promotes trust in God and requires you to care for your neighbors. Seek the company of others, especially people to whom you may be of service.

**❹ Remember, your Lord also confronted temptation.**
Jesus faced down temptation by telling the devil the truth, namely, only God is Lord. Consider using a contemporary version of Jesus' words: "God's in charge here, not you."

**❺ Tell the devil to go back to hell.**
Consider saying this: "You're right, Mr. Devil. I'm a sinner. Unfortunately, you have no power here. My Lord loves sinners and has forgiven me forever. There's nothing you can do about it. Go back to where you came from and quit bothering me!"

## Be Aware

- There are different kinds of temptation. Regardless of the type, temptation always involves a hidden voice whispering to you, "Whatever God says, you really need to trust me instead. I'm the only thing that can help you."

- Temptations try to make us trust in ourselves or in other things more than in God. When you realize this, you'll see that everything on the list above is just turning back to Jesus who died to show you how much you can trust him.

*Even Jesus faced temptation when the devil confronted him in the wilderness.*

# HOW TO CARE FOR THE SICK

While a trained and licensed physician must be sought to treat illness and injury, there is no malady that cannot be helped with faithful attention and prayer.

**❶ Assess the nature of the problem.**
Visit a local pharmacy if the illness is a simple one. Over-the-counter medications usually provide temporary relief until the body heals itself. If symptoms persist, the sick person should see a doctor and get a more detailed diagnosis.

**❷ Pray for them.**
Intercessory prayers are prayers made on someone else's behalf. Recent studies point to healing in hospitalized patients who have been prayed for—even when the sick were not aware of the prayers. Add the afflicted person to your church's prayer list.

**❸ Call in the elders.**
Prayer and emotional support from friends and family are vital parts of healing, living with illness, and facing death. Ask the pastor to assemble the church elders (leaders) for prayer and the laying on of hands.

Here's what the Bible says on this topic: "Is any one of you sick? He should call the elders of the church to pray over tim and anoint him with oil in the name of the Lord" (James 5:14).

## Be Aware

- Many people claim expertise in healing, from acupuncturists and herbalists to "faith healers" and psychics. Use caution and skepticism, but keep an open mind.

- Many people believe that much healing can be found in "comfort foods," such as homemade chicken soup.

- Those who attempt to diagnose and treat their own symptoms can often do more harm than good. When in doubt, always consult a pharmacist, doctor, or other medical professional.

*Gather friends, family, and church leaders to pray and lay hands on sick people.*

# HOW TO IDENTIFY AND AVOID EVIL

The devil delights in unnoticed evil. To this end, he employs a wide array of lies, disguises, and deceptions while attacking our relationships with God and each other. A sharp eye and vigilance are your best defense. Many Christians dislike the subject of evil, but some secretly cultivate extraordinary talent for rooting it out.

**❶ Know your enemy.**
Evil appears in many forms, most often using camouflage to present itself as kindly or friendly. Cruelty, hatred, violence, and exploitation are among the many forms evil can take, but it often masquerades as justice or something done "for their own good." Be alert to acts, people, and events that employ these methods, even if the eventual outcome appears to be good.

**❷ Proceed carefully and deliberately.**
Avoid rushing to conclusions. Use good judgment.

**❸ Take action to expose the evil.**
Evil relies on darkness. It wants to remain hidden and hates the light of truth. Things that suffer from public knowledge or scrutiny might be evil.

**❹ Be prepared to make a personal sacrifice.**
Fighting evil can be costly. A successful counterattack may require you to give up something you cherish. For Jesus, as for many of his followers, it was his life. Love is the foundation of sacrifice that combats evil.

**⑤ Stay vigilant.**

Evil's genius is shown in disguise, deception, and misdirection. Maintain your objectivity and apply the biblical measures of right and wrong you know to be correct.

*Evil employs deception and camouflage to accomplish its ends.*

# HOW TO AVOID GOSSIP

Gossip is among the most corrosive forces within a community and should be monitored closely. Discovery of gossip should be viewed as an opportunity to defend your neighbors' integrity, both gossiper and gossipee.

**1** Determine whether the conversation at hand qualifies as gossip.

- Gossip involves one party speaking about a second party to a third party.

- The person who is the topic of gossip is not a participant in the conversation.

- The tone of the conversation is often secretive or negative. Gasps and whispers are common.

- The facts expressed in a gossip conversation are often unsubstantiated and have been obtained second- or third-hand.

**2** Recall and heed Titus 3:2: "Speak evil of no one."

**3** Interject yourself into the conversation politely. Ask whether the gossiper(s) have spoken directly to the person about whom they are talking. If not, politely ask why. This may give some indication why they are gossiping.

**4** Make a statement of fact. Gossip withers in the face of truth. Make an attempt to parse out what is truly known from conjecture and supposition. State aloud that gossip is disrespectful and unfair.

*Avoid gossip. It undermines community and damages relationships.*

**⑤** Offer an alternative explanation based on fact. Describe other situations that cast the gossipee in a favorable light. Always try to give people the benefit of the doubt.

## Be Aware

- There is a fine line between helping and meddling. Pay close attention to your own motivations and the possible outcomes of your actions.

- Gossip injures both the gossiper and the person who is the subject of rumors.

- For further help, consult James 4:11.

# HOW TO BLESS SOMEONE

Blessings through history have had many purposes, often involving the passing of wealth or property from one person or generation to another. A Christian blessing is a declaration of the gospel of Jesus Christ to a specific individual—an affirmation that another person is claimed and loved by almighty God. Blessings should be dispensed liberally and with abandon.

❶ **Evaluate the need at hand.**
People have different needs at different times. When you perceive a need in which a blessing appears appropriate, take time to discern.

❷ **Use safe touch.**
Human touch is an affirmation with profound physical effects. Healing and emotional release are common. Make sure you use touch that is nonthreatening, respectful, and communicates the love of Christ.

❸ **Choose an appropriate way to give the blessing.**
- Position one or both hands on the person's head. Use a light touch, but one firm enough to let the person know that he or she is being blessed.

- Place one hand on the person's shoulder.

- Trace a cross on the person's forehead.

- Hold both of the person's hands in yours while making good eye contact.

**❹ Make a declaration of freedom.**

- Blessings are often most effective when the spoken word is employed.

- Consider ad-libbing a verbal blessing that speaks directly to the situation.

## Be Aware

- Indirect blessings are often appropriate. These include but are not limited to favors, prayers, kind words, consolation, a hot meal, shared laughter, and acceptance.

- Some cultures consider head-touching impolite or even rude, so always ask permission before making a blessing this way if there is any doubt.

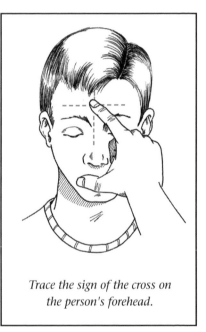

*Trace the sign of the cross on the person's forehead.*

# FIVE WAYS TO
# PUT GOD FIRST DAILY

**❶ Begin the day by opening the Bible.**
It's both a discipline and an acquired taste, but if you ask God to talk to you, He will. The Bible is one of God's primary tools.

**❷ Pray about your day.**
See what names, words, and situations float to the surface. God may want you to focus on those. As you pray, allow God to reshape and set your priorities.

**❸ Take stock of sins that might be keeping you from putting God first and repent.**

**❹ Remind yourself God has a purpose for you.**
Remember that life is not about being comfortable. The goal of life is to serve God and be part of what God is doing.

**❺ Be mindful of the "onionskin factor."**
The "onionskin factor" is the realization that everyday life has a lot in common with peeling an onion. You take off one skin and there is another skin beneath. Always there is another skin. Each day is a new opportunity to give your sins over to God and receive His grace and blessings.

# HOW TO RESOLVE INTERPERSONAL CONFLICT

Disagreements are part of life. They often occur when we forget that not everyone sees things the same way. Conflict should be viewed as an opportunity to grow, not a contest for domination.

**❶ Adopt a healthy attitude.**
Your frame of mind is critical. Approach the situation with forethought and calm. Prayer can be invaluable at this stage. Do not approach the other party when you're angry or upset.

**❷ Read Matthew 18:15-20 beforehand.**
Consult the Bible to orient your thinking. This is the model Jesus provided and can be used to call to mind an appropriate method.

**❸ Talk directly to the person involved.**
Avoid "triangulation." Talking about someone to a third party can make the conflict worse, as the person may feel that he or she is the subject of gossip. Speaking with the other person directly eliminates the danger and boosts the odds of a good outcome.

**❹ Express yourself without attacking.**
Using "I statements" can avoid casting the other person as the "bad guy" and inflaming the conflict. "I statements" are sentences beginning with phrases such as, "I feel …," or, "I'm uncomfortable when …"

**⑤ Keep "speaking the truth in love" (Ephesians 4:15) as your goal.**
Your "truth" may not be the other party's. Your objective is to discover and honor each other's "truth," not to put down the other person. Be ready to admit your own faults and mistakes.

**⑥ Seek out a third party to act as an impartial witness.**
If direct conversation doesn't resolve the conflict, locate someone both parties trust to sit in. This can help clarify your positions and bring understanding.

**⑦ Build toward forgiveness and a renewed friendship.**
Agree upon how you will communicate to prevent future misunderstandings.

## Be Aware

- Seemingly unrelated events in your or the other person's life may be playing an invisible role in the conflict at hand. Be ready to shift the focus to the real cause.

- You may not be able to resolve the conflict at this time, but don't give up on future opportunities.

*When two people aren't getting along, sometimes an impartial third person can help resolve the dispute.*

# HOW TO CONSOLE SOMEONE

Consolation is a gift from God. Christians in turn give it to others to build up the body of Christ and preserve it in times of trouble. (See 2 Corinthians 1:4-7.) Many Christians employ food as a helpful secondary means.

**❶ Listen first.**
Make it known that you're present and available.
When the person opens up, be quiet and attentive.

**❷ Be ready to help the person face grief and sadness, not avoid them.**
The object is to help the person name, understand, and work through his or her feelings, not gloss over them.

**❸ Avoid saying things to make yourself feel better.**
"I know exactly how you feel," is seldom true and trivializes the sufferer's pain. Even if you have experienced something similar, no experience is exactly the same. If there is nothing to say, simply be present with the person.

**❹ Show respect with honesty.**
Don't try to answer the mysteries of the universe or force your beliefs on the person. Be clear about the limitations of your abilities. Be ready to let some questions go unanswered. Consolation isn't about having all the answers, it's about bearing one another's burdens.

**❺ Don't put words in God's mouth.**
Avoid saying, "This is God's will," or, "This is part of God's plan." Unless you heard it straight from God, don't say it. Even if you believe such words to be true, saying them is seldom a consolation to a suffering person.

# HOW TO COPE WITH LOSS AND GRIEF

Christians sometimes downplay their losses by saying, "Well, it could be worse." This may provide only temporary relief at best. Any loss can cause pain, feelings of confusion, and uncertainty. These responses are normal.

**❶ Familiarize yourself with the stages of grief.**
Experts identify five: denial, anger, bargaining, depression, and acceptance. Some add hope as a sixth stage. Grieving persons cycle back and forth through the stages, sometimes experiencing two or three in a single day. This is normal.

**❷ Express your grief.**
Healthy ways may include crying, staring into space for extended periods, ruminating, shouting at the ceiling, and sudden napping. Laughing outbursts are also appropriate and should not be judged harshly.

**❸ Identify someone you trust to talk to.**
Available people can include a spouse, parents, relatives, friends, a pastor, a doctor, or a trained counselor. Many household pets also make good listeners and willing confidants.

**❹ Choose a personal way to memorialize the loss.**
Make a collage of photographs, offer a memorial donation to your church, or start a scrapbook of memories to honor the event. This helps you to begin to heal without getting stuck in your grief.

## Be Aware

- Many experts prescribe a self-giving activity, such as volunteering at a shelter or soup kitchen, as a means of facilitating a healthy grieving process.

- The pain immediately after suffering a loss is usually deep and intense. This will lessen with the passage of time.

- Anger, guilt, bitterness, and sadness are likely emotions.

- Short-term depression may occur in extreme cases. After experiencing a great loss, such as the death of a loved one, make an appointment with your family physician for a physical.

- Even Jesus cried when his friend Lazarus died (John 11:35).

*Even Jesus felt the loss of Lazarus when he died.*

Mary    Martha

# THE TOP 10 ATTRIBUTES TO LOOK FOR IN A SPOUSE

While no single personality trait can predict a compatible marriage, the following list frames the basic things to look for in a spouse. With all attributes, some differences can be the source of a couple's strength rather than a source of difficulty. Statistically, Christians appear to be about as successful at choosing a spouse as other people.

**❶ Similar values.**
Values that concern religious beliefs, life purpose, financial priorities, and children are a foundation on which to build the relationship. Contrary values tend to create discord.

**❷ Physical-energy and physical-space compatibility.**
Consider whether the person's energy level and physical-space needs work with yours. Also, the word *compatibility* can mean a complementary match of opposites, or it can denote a match based on strong similarities.

**❸ Physical and romantic compatibility.**
If the two of you have a similar degree of interest in or need for physical and romantic expression in your relationship, the chance of lifelong compatibility increases.

**❹ Intellectual parity.**
Communicating with someone who has a significantly different intelligence level or educational background can require extra effort.

**⑤ Emotional maturity.**

A lifelong relationship of mutual challenge and support often helps each person grow emotionally, but a lifetime spent waiting for someone to grow up could be more frustration than it's worth.

**⑥ Sense of humor.**

Sense of humor can provide an excellent measure of a person's personality and an important means to couple survival. If he or she doesn't get your jokes, you could be asking for trouble.

**⑦ Respect.**

Look for someone who listens to you without trying to control you. Look also for a healthy sense of self-respect.

**⑧ Trustworthiness.**

Seek out someone who is honest and acts with your best interests in mind—not only his or hers—and tries to learn from his or her mistakes.

**⑨ Forgiving.**

When you sincerely apologize to your spouse, he or she should try to work through and get beyond the problem rather than hold on to it. Once forgiven, past mistakes should not be raised, especially in conflict situations.

**⑩ Kindness.**

An attitude of consistent kindness may be the most critical attribute for a lifelong partnership.

## Be Aware

- If you live a long life, you probably will experience major changes that you cannot predict at age 15 or 25 or 35. Accepting this fact in advance can help you weather difficult times.

- Use all of your resources—intuition, emotions, and rational thought—to make the decision about a life partner.

- Family members and trusted friends can offer invaluable advice in this decision-making process and should be consulted.

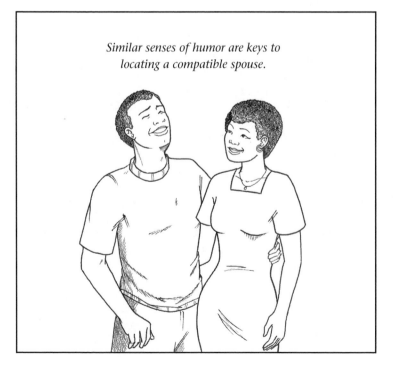

*Similar senses of humor are keys to locating a compatible spouse.*

# HOW TO KEEP CHRIST AT THE CENTER OF A MARRIAGE

A Christ-centered marriage is no accident. It takes work. While God supplies marriages with great attention and care, the couple, if they wish their marriage to bear the marks of Christ, must want it to be so and must be willing to make many sacrifices for a greater joy. A Christ-centered marriage is like a Christ-centered life.

**❶ Make every effort to avoid sexual sin even before getting married.**
Avoid exposing your future marriage to prior injury. Stay focused. Reject in-the-moment temptations in favor of achieving your goal of a lifelong, monogamous, Christ-centered marriage.

**❷ When possible, seek a partner who already knows Jesus as his or her Lord and Savior.**
Insofar as you are able to control with whom you fall in love, attempt to select persons of a like mind with regard to Christ. If either or both of you come to faith later on, post-wedding, a Christ-centered marriage is still possible and may even yield unique fruits of joy.

**❸ Ask God early on to give both of you the same heart.**
In prayer together, ask God to give you common desires and common direction. Most crucially, ask God to give both of you desires that fit where God wants you to go. This will help get things off on the right foot.

**❹ Pray together regularly.**

Even a lifetime of praying together does not inoculate against trouble, but it does give two people opportunity for discussion, mediation, and hope when things get difficult—as they surely will. *Note:* Maintaining this habit can become extremely difficult as time progresses; endeavor to persevere. With time, it will pay off.

**❺ Try always to keep a clean slate with the other person. Make it a part of your daily ritual together.**

Attempt to build a relationship in which you are unafraid to tell each other your innermost thoughts. Rather than your spouse questioning your humanity, you may find that he or she actually grows closer to you because you seek his or her help with a flaw and that you are serious about needing help.

**❻ Don't let the sun go down on your anger. Resolve to settle differences before they accumulate and become an unmanageable burden.**

This biblical mandate makes good sense. It is best not to let problems pile up. Consider using your daily prayer or devotional times as opportunities to confess and be done with wrongdoing.

**❼ Attend church together and reflect on God's presence as you encounter him outside of church.**

Provide yourselves time to be in awe of God and Christ in each other's company. Share Bible verses at unexpected times of the day. Go to the mountains and ask God to reveal His majesty. Give yourselves time to rest and don't always be quick to leave to do some other tasks.

⑧ Make laughter a priority.

No marriage can survive without humor, and a Christ-centered marriage is especially dependent on it. As your commitment to God can place you at odds with the culture around you, a healthy sense of humor is crucial. Laugh at yourself before you allow yourself to laugh at your spouse.

## Be Aware

- Keeping Christ at the center of a marriage means bringing the changes and troubles to Christ and to each other as the years progress.

- Choosing to place Christ at the center of your marriage is a willful act of defiance. More the norm are marriages that lack a center, or that center on the wrong things.

*Attending church together helps to keep Christ at the center of a marriage.*

# HOW TO BANISH THE DEVIL FROM YOUR PRESENCE

Since God loved the flesh so much as to redeem it by becoming flesh, Christians believe that the devil, by contrast, hates the flesh. Bodily acts, therefore, hold the power to send the devil packing. While the existence of a "personal" devil—a physical entity embodying pure evil—is part of the Christian tradition, many tend to withhold final judgment on specifics. Still, it's good to be prepared.

**❶ Laugh out loud.**

Laughter is abhorrent to the devil and should be indulged in frequently.

**❷ Make the sign of the cross.**

The devil hates the cross because that is where God's love for you is most evident.

**❸ Seek the company of other believers.**

Play games with children, attend worship, join a prayer team, host a dinner party, or locate a Bible study. Solitude can provide the devil an opportunity.

**❹ Serve those who have less than you.**

Resolve to volunteer your time to help those less fortunate than you. The devil is thwarted by the love of Christ in action.

**❺ Confess your sins.**

The devil is attracted to a guilty conscience. Confession clears the conscience and emboldens the believer.

**6** Break wind.

The devil (along with anyone else in the room) might well leave you alone. Though perhaps "gross," this act was a favorite of Protestant reformer Martin Luther.

**7** Consider what you might be doing to invite the devil into your life.

We invite the devil into our lives when our actions and values no longer center on Christ.

*Banish the devil by taking part in activities with others.*
*Avoid excessive solitude.*

# HOW TO IDENTIFY
# A POSSESSED PERSON

*Note:* Advancements in medical science have made it easier to distinguish cases of possession from mental illness— a critical difference! The authors of Scripture, both Old and New Testament, saw evil as very real. Demons are mentioned more than 80 times in the New Testament alone, and today our most learned pastors and countless believers maintain that their influence is still palpable. Here are some guidelines for recognizing signs of possession by demons (also described as fallen angels).

**❶ Physical ailments not linked to wounds or direct medical causes.**

These may include a loss of the ability to speak (Matthew 9:32-34), blindness (Matthew 12:22), seizures (Matthew 4:24), convulsions (Mark 9:14-29), or being disabled for years (Luke 13:11-17).

**❷ Superhuman strength, self-wounding behavior, and crying out.**

Mark 5:1-20 describes in detail the symptoms of a man in the country of the Gerasenes. This poor fellow lived among the tombstones, and his strength was such that chains and other men could not subdue him; he also gashed himself with stones and wailed aloud. Just as his symptoms were multiple, so were his demons: "My name is Legion, for we are many." Jesus cured the man by casting the foul spirits into a herd of swine. (Also see Matthew 8 and Luke 8.)

**❸** Abrupt personality changes.

After his rebellion against God, King Saul was vexed by an evil spirit (1 Samuel 16; 18-19), leading to depressed moods and increased signs of aggression—including a willingness to murder David, God's next anointed king of Israel.

**❹** Unprovoked acts of betrayal.

The most dramatic example is in Luke 22:3, where Satan possesses Judas, causing the disciple to turn against Jesus. In a typical betrayal, the perpetrator seeks revenge, justice, or to satisfy a growing thirst for power. Yet these enticements do not motivate Judas.

## Be Aware

- While it is the sign of mature faith to take evil seriously, it takes equal maturity to refrain from rushing to judgment! Attributing any of the above symptoms to demon possession without first taking time to pray, consult faith elders, or wrestle with the "diagnosis" can be akin to curing a headache by chopping off the sufferer's head.

- The New Testament DOES NOT ascribe all sickness to demons or evil spirits! It goes to great lengths to stress that followers of Christ need not live in fear of becoming possessed by demons.

# How to Identify a Possessed Person

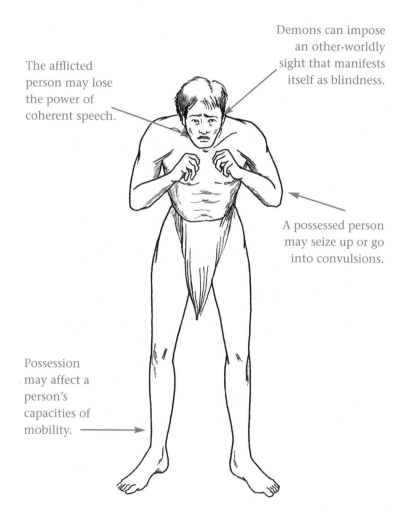

Demons can impose an other-worldly sight that manifests itself as blindness.

The afflicted person may lose the power of coherent speech.

A possessed person may seize up or go into convulsions.

Possession may affect a person's capacities of mobility.

# HOW TO IDENTIFY SOMEONE FILLED WITH THE HOLY SPIRIT

Before he ascended to the Father, Jesus promised that the Holy Spirit would come to each of his followers. The Holy Spirit may choose to enter a person's life in a variety of ways, and while the Holy Spirit may be invoked and even sought, only God can decide how and when someone will receive the Holy Spirit. When discerning the presence of the Holy Spirit, look for one or more of the following.

**❶ Tongues of flames may rest upon the spirit-filled person.**
This is unusual, but not impossible. Read Acts 2:3-4.

**❷ The person proclaims Jesus as Lord in both word and deed.**
No one can proclaim Jesus as Lord without the Holy Spirit. Read 1 Corinthians 12:3.

**❸ The person exhibits gifts of the Holy Spirit.**
1 Corinthians 12:1-13 lists a variety of spiritual gifts. Spiritual gifts surveys can also help a Spirit-filled person identify their own gifts and those of others.

**❹ The person's spiritual gifts bear fruit in the Christian community.**
The community is built up by the use of the spiritual gifts of the spirit-filled person. Read Galatians 5:16-26 for a list of both works of the flesh and fruits of the spirit.

**⑤ A person recently filled with the Holy Spirit may experience radical change in the way he or she lives.**
The Holy Spirit transforms lives. Read about Paul's transformation in Acts 9:1-22.

**⑥ Spirit-filled people are difficult to restrain from evangelistic activity.**
The Spirit so fills one's life as to spill over constantly. Look for constant witnessing to Jesus Christ as Lord.

## Be Aware

- Not everyone who claims to be filled with the Holy Spirit actually is. The Bible warns against succumbing to "false prophets" and others looking to steal the Spirit's thunder.

- The Holy Spirit does not bless people for their own personal gain, but for the building up of the community of Christ. A Spirit-filled person is not conceited or boastful.

- Human sin can interfere with the presence of the Holy Spirit, but it cannot separate a person from the love of God in Christ Jesus.

- In cases where the Spirit's presence is uncertain, seek the assistance of someone blessed with the gift of discernment of gifts.

- The Holy Spirit may enter your life or someone else's life at any time. Remain alert.

# How to Identify
## Someone Filled with the Holy Spirit

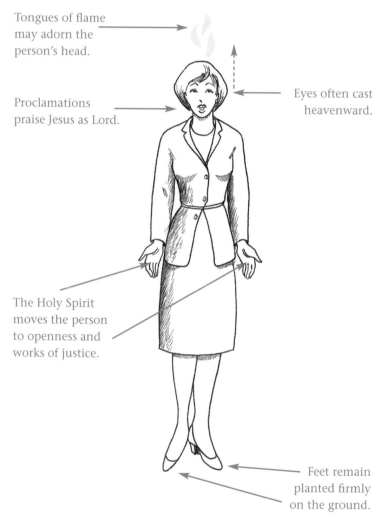

Tongues of flame may adorn the person's head.

Proclamations praise Jesus as Lord.

Eyes often cast heavenward.

The Holy Spirit moves the person to openness and works of justice.

Feet remain planted firmly on the ground.

# HOW TO IDENTIFY AN ANGEL

The word *angel* means "messenger" in both the Hebrew of the Old Testament and the Greek of the New Testament. In the Bible, God uses angels to communicate with people—to advise, call, protect, warn, judge, kill, bless, instruct, comfort, make birth announcements, and bring good news to them. When an angel shows up, somebody is in for an awe-inspiring, bone-rattling, life-changing experience. Here's how to be sure you're dealing with the real thing.

**1** Try to determine whether God might send an angel in those specific circumstances or whether you might be imagining things.

Finding a lost wallet and someone opening a door for you when you have your arms full probably don't qualify as angelic encounters. Be careful not to diminish an angel's work in your life by confusing it with made-up encounters or attributing everyday coincidences or kindnesses to an angel.

**2** Listen for a godly message.

In the Bible, God almost never sends an angel without sending a message. Keep in mind that God's messages sometimes include judgment and wrath as well as comfort, grace, and healing. Look also for prophecies of impending future events.

**3** Discern which type of angel you might be dealing with.

- *Old Testament angels:* Encounters with these angels are sometimes bizarre and even hazardous, but also occasionally playful. You might get your hip knocked out of its socket (Genesis 32:25) or your foot crushed (Numbers 22:25), but you might also receive good culinary advice (Judges 6:20) or protection from hungry lions (Daniel 6:22).

- **New Testament angels:** These messengers appear chiefly to deliver good news and don't seem to get too involved in matters physically, though they reserve the right to do so when necessary (Matthew 28:2; John 5:4).

- **Modern-day angels:** These angels seem to bring primarily feelings of happiness, protection, and preservation, though very seldom a message. The discrepancy with the biblical models has caused some to question the authenticity of some modern-day encounters.

④ Take time to grapple with your angelic encounter before making final judgments and announcing it to everyone.
If it truly was an angelic encounter, God will make that clear over time, perhaps even sending the angel for repeat visits until you get the message. If not, blabbing about a questionable event might make you look like a kook.

## Be Aware

- Avoid confusing an angel with God. Angels sometimes appear subtly and slip into roles the Bible attributes only to God. Angels cannot deliver salvation, grace, or forgiveness of sins.

- Hunches, intuition, and a "sixth sense" are not signs of an angelic message from God. If an angel brings a message, you'll know it.

- Angels are not believed to use telepathy, coincidence, or other cryptic signals to communicate, as in some modern-day reports. God-sent angels typically speak their messages out loud.

# How to Identify an Angel

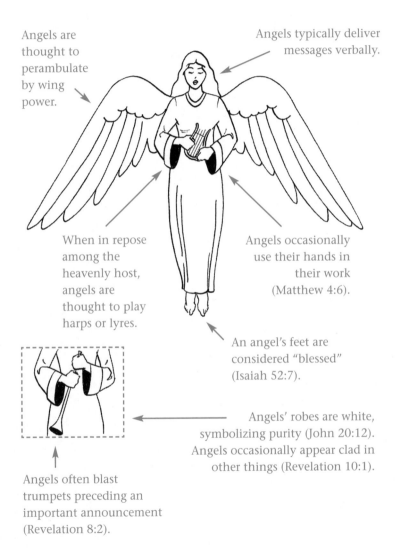

Angels are thought to perambulate by wing power.

Angels typically deliver messages verbally.

When in repose among the heavenly host, angels are thought to play harps or lyres.

Angels occasionally use their hands in their work (Matthew 4:6).

An angel's feet are considered "blessed" (Isaiah 52:7).

Angels' robes are white, symbolizing purity (John 20:12). Angels occasionally appear clad in other things (Revelation 10:1).

Angels often blast trumpets preceding an important announcement (Revelation 8:2).

# *BIBLE STUFF*

Written down by many people over hundreds of years, the Bible is more like a portable bookshelf than one book by itself. And because the Bible is God's Word, people often feel overwhelmed when they try to read it.

This section includes:

- Helpful information about when, where, and why people wrote the 66 books within the Bible. (It didn't all come together at once.)

- Tips for reading and understanding the Bible—how it's organized and what it says.

- Some of the most mystifying, hair-raising, and just plain off-the-wall stories in the Bible.

# COMMON TRANSLATIONS OF THE BIBLE

| Translation | Grade Level* | Theological Affiliation | Year Released | Special Features |
|---|---|---|---|---|
| King James Version | 12.0 | Church of England, conservative and evangelical | 1611 | Poetic style using Elizabethan English. Most widely used translation for centuries. |
| New American Standard Bible | 11.0 | Conservative and evangelical | 1971; updated, 1995 | Revision of the 1901 American Standard Version into contemporary language. |
| New Revised Standard Version | 8.1 | Mainline and interconfessional | 1989 | Updated version of the Revised Standard Version. |
| New King James Version | 8.0 | Transnational, transdenominational, conservative, and evangelical | 1982 | Updates the King James text into contemporary language. |
| New International Version | 7.8 | Transnational, transdenominational, conservative, and evangelical | 1978; revised, 1984 | Popular modern-language version. Attempts to balance literal and dynamic translation methods. |
| Today's English Version (also called the Good News Bible) | 7.3 | Evangelical and interconfessional | 1976 | Noted for its freshness of language. |

| Version | Grade Level* | Tradition | Date | Description |
| --- | --- | --- | --- | --- |
| New American Bible | 6.6 | Roman Catholic | 1970; revised NT, 1986; revised Psalms, 1991 | Official translation of the Roman Catholic Church in the United States. |
| New Living Translation | 6.4 | Evangelical | 1996 | A meaning-for-meaning translation. Successor to the Living Bible. |
| New Century Version | 5.6 | Conservative and evangelical | 1988; revised, 1991 | Follows the Living Word Vocabulary. |
| Contemporary English Version | 5.4 | Conservative, evangelical, mainline | 1995 | Easy-to-read English for new Bible readers. |
| The Message | 4.8, from NT samples | Evangelical | 2002 | An expressive paraphrase of the Bible. |

*The grade level on which the text is written, using Dale-chall, Fry, Raygor, and Spache Formulas.

## Bible classifications

**Apocrypha Bible:** Contains certain books that Protestants don't consider canonical. Most of these OT books are accepted by the Roman Catholic Church.

**Children's Bible:** Includes illustrations and other study aids that are especially helpful for children.

**Concordance Bible:** Lists places in the Bible where key words are found.

**Red Letter Bible:** The words spoken by Christ appear in red.

**Reference Bible:** Pages include references to other Bible passages on the same subject.

**Self-Proclaiming Bible:** Diacritical marks (as in a dictionary) appear above difficult names and words to help with the pronunciation.

**Text Bible:** Contains text without footnotes or column references. May include maps, illustrations, and other helpful material.

# HOW TO READ THE BIBLE

The Bible is a collection of 66 separate books gathered together over hundreds of years and thousands of miles. Divided into the Old Testament (Hebrew language) and the New Testament (Greek language), these writings have many authors and take many forms.

The Bible includes histories, stories, prophecies, poetry, songs, teachings, and laws, to name a few. Christians believe the Bible is the story of God's relationship with humankind and a powerful way that God speaks to people.

**❶ Determine your purpose for reading.**
Clarify in your own mind what you hope to gain. Your motivations should be well intentioned, such as to seek information, to gain a deeper understanding of God and yourself, or to enrich your faith. Pray for insight before every reading time.

*Commit to reading the Bible daily.*

❷ **Resolve to read daily.** Commit to a daily regimen of Bible reading. Make it a part of your routine until it becomes an unbreakable habit.

chapter number

→

**Proverbs 26:11**

↗ ↑

book name

verse number

❸ **Master the mechanics.**
- Memorize the books of the Bible in order.

- Familiarize yourself with the introductory material. Many Bible translations include helpful information at the front of the Bible and at the beginning of each book.

- The books are broken down into chapters and verses. Locate the beginning of a book by using the Bible's table of contents. Follow the numerical chapter numbers; these are usually in large type. Verses are likewise numbered in order within each chapter. Simply run your finger down the page until you locate the verse number you're looking for.

- If your Bible contains maps (usually in the back), consult them when cities, mountains, or seas are mentioned in your reading.

❹ **Befriend the written text.**
Read with a pen or pencil in hand and underline passages of interest. Look up unfamiliar words in a dictionary. Write notes in the margins when necessary.

❺ **Practice reading from the Bible out loud.**

# HOW TO MEMORIZE A BIBLE VERSE

Memorizing Scripture is an ancient faith practice. Its value is often mentioned by people who have, in crisis situations, remembered comforting or reassuring passages coming to mind, sometimes decades after first memorizing them. There are three common methods of memorization.

## Method 1: Memorize with Music

Choose a verse that is special for you. It is more difficult to remember something that doesn't make sense to you or that lacks meaning.

*Write the verse out longhand several dozen times.*

❶ **Choose a familiar tune.** Pick something catchy and repetitious.

❷ **Add the words from the Bible verse to your tune.** Mix up the words a bit, if necessary. Memorizing a verse "word for word" isn't always as important as learning the message of the verse.

❸ **Mark the verse in your Bible.** This will help you find it again later on. Consider highlighting or underlining it.

❹ **Make the words rhyme,** if possible.

## Method 2: The Three S's (See it, Say it, Script it)

This method works on the principle of multisensory reinforcement. The brain creates many more neural pathways to a memory through sight, speech, and manipulation (writing) than just one of these, so recall is quicker and easier.

**1** Write the verse on index cards in large print.
Post the cards in places you regularly look, such as the refrigerator door or bathroom mirror.

**2** Say the verse out loud.
Repeat the verse 10 times to yourself every time you notice one of your index cards.

**3** Write the verse down.

**4** Try saying and writing the verse at the same time.
Repeat.

## Method 3: Old-Fashioned Memorization

Attempt this method only if you consider yourself to be "old school" or if the other methods fail.

**1** Write the verse out by hand on paper.
A whiteboard can work extremely well, also. Consider writing it as many as 100 times. Repeat this process until you can recite the verse flawlessly.

**2** Don't get up until you've memorized the verse.
Open your Bible to the appropriate verse, sit down in front of it, and don't get up, eat, sleep, or use the bathroom until you can recite it flawlessly.

**3** Enlist a family member or friend to help you.
Have them read along with you and prompt you when you get stuck.

# HOW TO REMEMBER THE BOOKS OF THE BIBLE

Aside from rote memorization, putting the names of the books to music can help commit them to memory. Many songwriters have scored such songs over the centuries, and we suggest coming up with your own tune to further embed the names in your mind. One old-timey version appears on page 139.

*Memorizing Scripture is an ancient faith practice. It takes a little concentration.*

# The Books of the Bible

A.P.G.

Alfred P. Gibbs, 1931

Gen- e - sis, Ex-o-dus, Le - vit-i-cus, Num- bers, Deu-ter-on-o - my,
Prov - erbs,Ec-cle - si - as - tes, Song of Sol - o - mon,
Mat - thew, Mark, Luke, John, Acts, Ro-mans,Co-rin - thi - ans,

Josh-ua, Judg-es, Ruth and First and Sec-ond Sam- u - el;
I - sa-iah,Jer-e-mi-ah, Lam-en - ta - tions, E - ze-ki-el, Dan-iel,Ho - s-ea;
Ga - la - tians,E-phe-si-ans,Phi-lip-pi-ans,Co-los-sians,Thes-sa - lo - ni - ans;

First and Sec - ond Kings and First and Sec - ond Chron- i - cles,
Jo-el, A-mos,O - ba-di-ah, Jo-nah, Mi-cah, Na-hum, Ha - bak - kuk,
Tim-o-thy, Ti - tus, and Phi - le-mon, He-brews,and then James,

Ez - ra, Ne-he-mi-ah, Es - ther, Job, and now the Book of Psalms;
Zeph-a-ni-ah, Hag - ga-i, Zech - a - ri-ah and then comes Mal-a - chi;
Pe - ter, John, Jude, Rev-e - la - tion, ends the Word of God.

Note: The song does not specifically name the books of 2 Corinthians, 2 Thessalonians, 2 Timothy, 2 Peter, 2 John, and 3 John.

# THE TOP FIVE
# BIBLE BEDTIME STORIES

While the Bible is most often used in corporate worship, it nonetheless contains powerful stories that shine and sparkle in different ways as Christians read and reread them in their own homes. Consider making Bible reading a daily ritual.

## The Top Five Bible Bedtime Stories for Adults

**❶ Song of Songs.** Song of Songs is a love poem and contains passages many regard as saucy. Consider reading from this book only if you are married.

**❷ Genesis and Exodus, any chapter.** These stories read like cinematic sagas, and the characters are as flawed and compelling as the rest of us.

**❸ Jonah.**

A short read, but great for anyone trying to escape from something.

**❹ Esther.**

Beautiful women, nasty villains, lavish banquets. Bible stories at their best.

**❺ Ruth.**

A story of loyalty, love, and how small struggles can lead to God's big works.

## The Top Five Bible Bedtime Stories for Kids

**❶ David and Goliath. (1 Samuel 17).**

The perennial favorite. The diminutive, plucky underdog beats the experienced warrior.

**❷ Peter's escape from prison (Acts 12).**
Kids love the clever plot twists.

**❸ Paul's preaching starts a riot (Acts 19:23).**

The power of the gospel to disrupt everyday life is alive in this story. Adults and kids need to hear it read with verve and passion.

**❹ The new heaven and new earth (Revelation 21-22).**

Read it aloud for great visual appeal and a beautiful, phantasmagorical vision of the gospel come to life.

**❺ God's promise to Abram (Genesis 15).**

This story is a blueprint for the rest of the Bible's story of salvation: God makes lavish promises—and delivers on them—in the face of incalculable odds and against every human expectation, even of those to whom he makes the promises.

*Kids love the dramatic story of Peter's prison break in Acts 12.*

## Be Aware

- The stories of Noah and Jonah are also perennial favorites. Be cautious not to use them and neglect other rich and entertaining stories.

# THE 12 TRIBES OF ISRAEL AND WHAT HAPPENED TO THEM

In Bible times, a "tribe" was a way of organizing society. The 12 tribes were named for the sons of Jacob (whose name God later changed to Israel). Tribal membership came from being descended from a common ancestor and defined whom you could marry, where your animals could graze or find water, with whom and when you worshiped God, and—most importantly—where you lived.

Israel had four layers of social organization.

*Note:* Some of the larger clans may have been larger than certain small tribes.

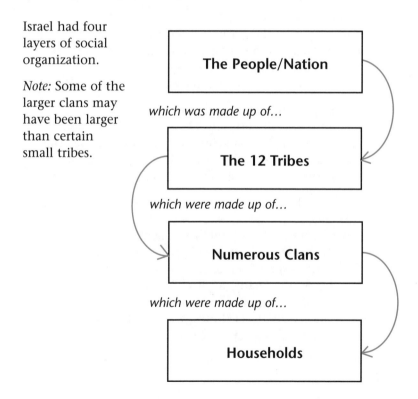

**The People/Nation**

*which was made up of…*

**The 12 Tribes**

*which were made up of…*

**Numerous Clans**

*which were made up of…*

**Households**

**❶ The 12 Tribes of Israel before Israel had Kings**
After they entered the promised land, God gave each
of the tribes (except Levi, see below) a territory in which
to live. Two and a half tribes settled east of the Jordan
River, while the rest settled west of the river.

**❷ During the monarchy.**
About 1000 B.C., Israel decided to have human kings.
During this time, the tribes continued to function on the
local level but relinquished some of their independence
to the kings, who chose Jerusalem as their capital.

**❸ After the kingdom split.**
About 922 B.C., the nation split in two. The northern
10 tribes split from Jerusalem and called their country
"Israel." The southern tribes of Benjamin and Judah
stayed loyal to Jerusalem and took the name "Judah."

**❹ The northern tribes' fate.**
The northern tribes survived as a nation until about
722 B.C., when Assyria defeated them and marched the
survivors away from their land. Some call the exiled
tribes "the lost tribes of Israel," because they disappeared
from history.

**❺ The southern tribes' fate.**
The southern tribes of Judah and Benjamin were
defeated about 586 B.C. Some Judeans were taken into
exile, others spread out to live in other countries.
Fifty years later, many of the exiles returned, but many
chose to live far from Jerusalem. The "Jewish" people
descended from these "Judeans." *Note:* The Levites also
survived, because they were split among all of the tribes.

# The 12 Tribes

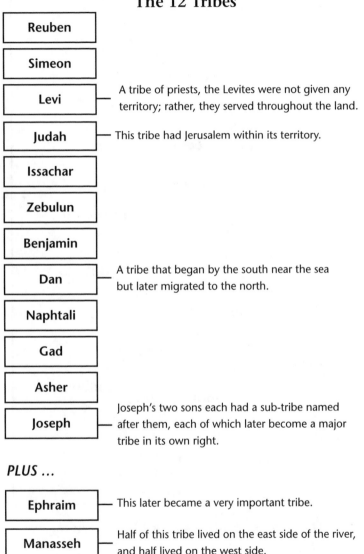

**Reuben**

**Simeon**

**Levi** — A tribe of priests, the Levites were not given any territory; rather, they served throughout the land.

**Judah** — This tribe had Jerusalem within its territory.

**Issachar**

**Zebulun**

**Benjamin**

**Dan** — A tribe that began by the south near the sea but later migrated to the north.

**Naphtali**

**Gad**

**Asher**

**Joseph** — Joseph's two sons each had a sub-tribe named after them, each of which later become a major tribe in its own right.

*PLUS ...*

**Ephraim** — This later became a very important tribe.

**Manasseh** — Half of this tribe lived on the east side of the river, and half lived on the west side.

*This map shows the locations of the 12 Tribes of Israel.*

# HOW TO IDENTIFY A PROPHET

A prophet is a messenger who receives a word from God and delivers it to a specific community. Often the message is a warning, an attempt to bring the people back on track with God. Identifying a prophet is no easy task; false prophets abound. However, there are characteristics of true prophets that can be used to assess the message and the messenger.

**❶ Prophets tend initially to resist their calling and vocation, due to its lonely and dangerous nature.**
Nobody signs up to be a prophet. If someone actually wants the job, he or she probably is not right for it. Look for a reticence to accept the call, at least at first.

**❷ Consider the nature of the times in which the prophet appears.**
Prophets often appear during times of crisis and uncertainty, or when the people have turned away from the Lord.

**❸ A prophet's message must conform to a previous revelation from God.**
God made clear what is expected of the people in the law. The prophet's message will be consistent with God's directives: doing justice, loving kindness, walking humbly with God (Micah 6:8), keeping the Commandments, remembering the poor, and so on.

**❹ Prophets nail the message and speak the truth.**
"If what a prophet proclaims in the name of the LORD does not take place or come true, that is a message the LORD has not spoken. That prophet has spoken presumptuously" (Deuteronomy 18:22).

**⑤ Avoid heeding prophets with a feel-good message.**
Prophecy seldom conveys a "job well done" message from the Lord. Warnings may include threats of death, disaster, pain, and suffering. (See 2 Chronicles 34:22-24 and Isaiah 38:1.)

**⑥ Prophets are without honor in their own country.**
You won't find many prophets in the "in" crowd. Recipients of the prophet's message from God typically adopt a "kill the messenger" attitude and often succeed. (See John 4:44.)

**⑦ Prophets generally practice poor hygiene.**
Physical characteristics of a prophet may include bad hair, locust breath, and honey stains. Check the fabrics: look for goat hair, animal skins, and other natural, breathable blends.

**⑧ Look for signs of poverty and hunger in a prophet.**
No one ever got rich prophesying for the Lord, as it often amounts to biting the hand that feeds him or her. A well-fed prophet probably sits too often at the king's table and delivers a salubrious message to the wealthy.

# How to Identify a Prophet

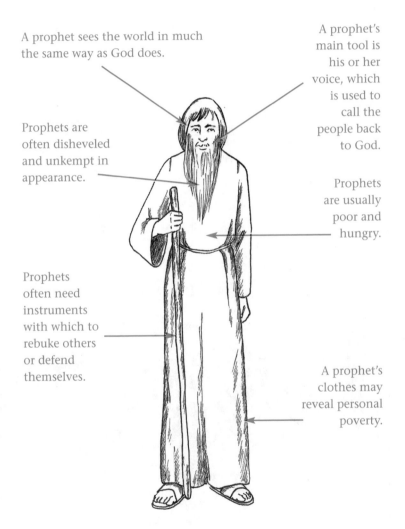

A prophet sees the world in much the same way as God does.

A prophet's main tool is his or her voice, which is used to call the people back to God.

Prophets are often disheveled and unkempt in appearance.

Prophets are usually poor and hungry.

Prophets often need instruments with which to rebuke others or defend themselves.

A prophet's clothes may reveal personal poverty.

# WHAT THE PROPHETS SAW

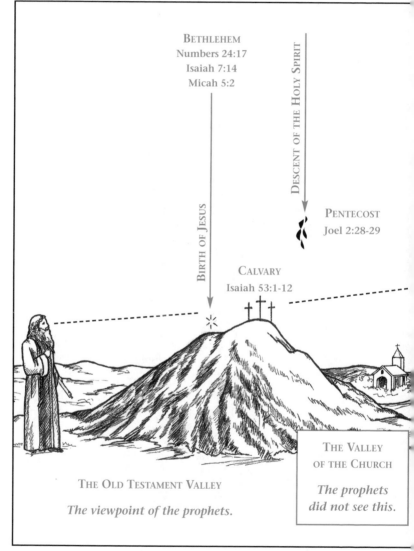

BETHLEHEM
Numbers 24:17
Isaiah 7:14
Micah 5:2

DESCENT OF THE HOLY SPIRIT

BIRTH OF JESUS

PENTECOST
Joel 2:28-29

CALVARY
Isaiah 53:1-12

THE VALLEY
OF THE CHURCH

*The prophets
did not see this.*

THE OLD TESTAMENT VALLEY

*The viewpoint of the prophets.*

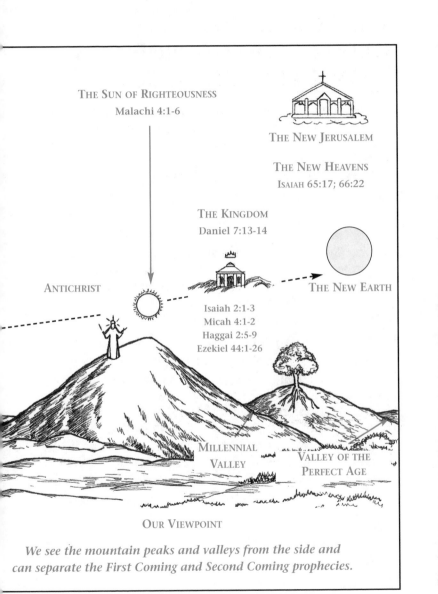

THE SUN OF RIGHTEOUSNESS
Malachi 4:1-6

THE NEW JERUSALEM

THE NEW HEAVENS
ISAIAH 65:17; 66:22

THE KINGDOM
Daniel 7:13-14

ANTICHRIST

THE NEW EARTH

Isaiah 2:1-3
Micah 4:1-2
Haggai 2:5-9
Ezekiel 44:1-26

MILLENNIAL
VALLEY

VALLEY OF THE
PERFECT AGE

OUR VIEWPOINT

*We see the mountain peaks and valleys from the side and can separate the First Coming and Second Coming prophecies.*

# THE TOP SEVEN OLD TESTAMENT PROPHETS AND THEIR MESSAGES

A prophet didn't so much predict the future as play the role of a messenger from God—with messages about the present. The prophets brought messages of hope and judgment, messages of warning and comfort, messages that promised deliverance, and messages that called people to repent.

**❶ Samuel.**
Samuel was a prophet during the time Israel chose a human king. Until that time, God had been the people's king. Samuel warned against human kings, citing the fact that God had been a pretty good king and that human kings hanker after high taxes, big harems, and violent wars. (See 1 Samuel 8.)

**❷ Nathan.**
Nathan was God's prophet after Samuel, during the reign of David. David got another man's wife, Bathsheba, pregnant, then covered it up by putting the husband, Uriah, in battle where he would die. This angered God, so Nathan told David a story about a farmer who had 10,000 sheep, but when he threw a party, the farmer instead killed his neighbor's one pet sheep. David flared up in anger at the farmer and said, "The man who did this deserves to die!" Nathan said, "You are the man!" (See 2 Samuel 11–12.)

**3** Elijah.

Elijah lived at a time when the people of Israel thought they could worship the Lord one day, Baal the next, Asherah the day after, and a few more gods on the off days. Elijah said, "No, you can't limp along on two opinions, you have to choose one—and there is only one real God: The Lord!" (See 1 Kings 18 and 21.)

**4** Amos.

Amos was a farmer and not really a prophet at all— and yet God had him deliver this message to the people: "You know what makes God angry? God gets angry when the poor suffer, when people abuse each other, when the wealthy ignore the unfortunate. You know what makes God happy? What makes God happy is when justice is the way we live every day." (See Amos 5:10-13, 21-24; and Micah 6:1-8.)

**5** Hosea.

Hosea chose to act out his message to God's people. He married a prostitute named Gomer, and told the people: "God is like someone who has married a prostitute—we are like an unfaithful spouse. We keep running from God, following other gods and filling our lives with things other than God. But like a faithful spouse, God will win us back, God will follow us anywhere, God loves us." (See Hosea 1-3.)

**❻ Isaiah.**

Isaiah prophesied in Jerusalem around 740–689 B.C. He spent a great deal of time near the kings who lived there. Sometimes they thirsted for his messages, and sometimes they avoided his messages. But Isaiah's message was consistent: Have faith, trust God. Isaiah also promised that one day God would send the ideal king to rule the chosen people. (See Isaiah 1, 5, and 11.)

**❼ Jeremiah.**

Jeremiah prophesied at a sad time, about 100 years after Isaiah. During Jeremiah's time, the people said, "All we have to do is have faith and trust God, and God will save us—Isaiah said so!" Jeremiah begged, pleaded, screamed, and shouted, "But do not forget that to have faith also means obeying God's law and dealing justly with your neighbors—Isaiah said so!" The people did not listen to Jeremiah. In fact, they locked him in the stockades, abused him, threw him down a well, and imprisoned him. When Jerusalem was destroyed, Jeremiah said, "God still loves you and you are still God's people—God will make a new covenant with you."

# THE TOP 10 BIBLE VILLAINS

**❶ Satan.**

The Evil One is known by many names in the Bible and appears many places, but the devil's purpose is always the same: To disrupt and confuse people so they turn from God and seek to become their own gods. This Bible villain is still active today.

**❷ The serpent.**

In Eden, the serpent succeeded in tempting Adam and Eve to eat from the tree of the knowledge of good and evil (Genesis 3:1-7). As a result, sin entered creation. If it weren't for the serpent, we'd all still be walking around naked, eating fresh fruit, and living forever.

**❸ Pharaoh (probably Seti I or Rameses II).**

The notorious Pharaoh from the book of Exodus enslaved the Israelites. Moses eventually begged him to "Let my people go," but Pharaoh hardened his heart and refused. Ten nasty plagues later, Pharaoh relented, but then changed his mind again. In the end, with his army at the bottom of the sea, Pharaoh finally gave his slaves up to the wilderness.

**❹ Goliath.**

"The Philistine of Gath," who stood six cubits in height (about nine feet tall), was sent to fight David, still a downy-headed youth of 15. Goliath was a fighting champion known for killing people, but David drilled Goliath in the head with a rock from his sling and gave God the glory (1 Samuel 17).

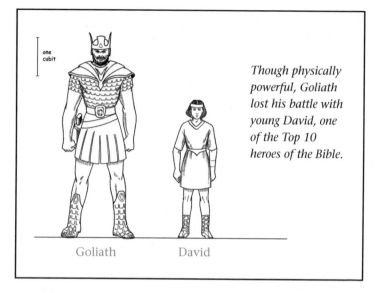

one cubit

Goliath          David

*Though physically powerful, Goliath lost his battle with young David, one of the Top 10 heroes of the Bible.*

**❺ Jezebel.**

King Ahab of Judah's wife and a follower of the false god Baal, Jezebel led her husband away from God and tried to kill off the prophets of the Lord. Elijah the prophet, however, was on the scene. He shamed Jezebel's false prophets and killed them (1 Kings 18:40).

**❻ King Herod.**

Afraid of any potential threat to his power, upon hearing about the birth of the Messiah in Bethlehem Herod sent the Wise Men to pinpoint his location. Awestruck by the Savior in the cradle, the Wise Men went home by a different route and avoided Herod. In a rage, he ordered the murder of every child two years of age or younger in the vicinity of Bethlehem. The baby Messiah escaped with his parents to Egypt (Matthew 2:14-15).

**7** The Pharisees, Sadducees, and Scribes.
They dogged Jesus throughout his ministry, alternately challenging his authority and being awed by his power. It was their leadership, with the consent and blessing of the people and the Roman government, that brought Jesus to trial and execution.

**8** Judas.
One of Jesus' original disciples, Judas earned 30 pieces of silver by betraying his Lord over to the authorities. He accomplished this by leading the soldiers into the garden of Gethsemane where he revealed Jesus with a kiss (Matthew 26–27).

**9** Pontius Pilate.
The consummate politician, the Roman governor chose to preserve his own bloated status by giving the people what they wanted: Jesus' crucifixion. He washed his hands to signify self-absolution, but bloodied them instead.

**10** God's people.
They whine, they sin, they turn their backs on God over and over again. When given freedom, they blow it. When preached repentance by God's prophets, they stone them. When offered a Savior, they kill him. In the end, it must be admitted, God's people—us!—don't really shine. Only by God's grace and the gift of faith in Jesus Christ do we have hope.

# THE TOP 10 BIBLE HEROES

The Bible is filled with typical examples of heroism, but another kind of hero inhabits the pages of the Bible—those people who, against all odds, follow God no matter the outcome. These are heroes of faith.

 **Noah.**

In the face of ridicule from others, Noah trusted God when God chose him to build an ark to save a remnant of humanity from destruction. Noah's trust became part of a covenant with God.

*Noah trusted God, even though others made fun of him. By following God's instructions and building a great ark, Noah and his family survived the flood (Genesis 6–10).*

**❷ Abraham and Sarah.**
In extreme old age, Abraham and Sarah answered God's call to leave their home and travel to a strange land, where they became the parents of God's people.

**❸ Moses.**
Moses, a man with a speech impediment, challenged the Egyptian powers to deliver God's people from bondage. He led a rebellious and contrary people for 40 years through the wilderness and gave them God's law.

**❹ Rahab.**
A prostitute who helped Israel conquer the promised land, Rahab was the great-grandmother of King David, and thus a part of the family of Jesus himself.

**❺ David.**
Great King David, the youngest and smallest member of his family, defeated great enemies, turning Israel into a world power. He wrote psalms, led armies, and confessed his sins to the Lord.

**❻ Mary and Joseph.**
These humble peasants responded to God's call to be the parents of the Messiah, although the call came through a pregnancy that was not the result of marriage.

**❼ The Canaanite woman.**
Desperate for her daughter's health, the Canaanite woman challenged Jesus regarding women and race by claiming God's love for all people (Matthew 15:21-28). Because of this, Jesus praised her faith.

**8** Peter.

Peter was a man quick to speak but slow to think. At Jesus' trial, Peter denied ever having known him. But in the power of forgiveness and through Christ's appointment, Peter became a leader in the early church.

**9** Saul/Paul.

Originally an enemy and persecutor of Christians, Paul experienced a powerful vision of Jesus, converted, and became the greatest missionary the church has ever known.

**10** Phoebe.

A contemporary of Paul's, Phoebe is believed to have delivered the book of Romans after traveling some 800 miles from Cenchrea near Corinth to Rome. A wealthy woman, she used her influence to travel, protect other believers, and to host worship services in her home.

*Phoebe is believed to have delivered the book of Romans after traveling 800 miles.*

# HOW TO SURVIVE AN OLD TESTAMENT PLAGUE

In the Bible, God sent plagues as a form of judgment. Plagues took different forms—disease, natural disasters, even military defeats. The most well-known plagues are the 10 plagues sent against Egypt when Pharaoh would not free God's people (blood, frogs, gnats, flies, livestock pestilence, boils, hail, locusts, darkness, the death of firstborn males).

But the Bible describes many more. God sent plagues against individuals (such as Pharaoh, see Genesis 12:17), foreign nations (such as the Philistines, see 1 Samuel 5:6), and God's chosen nation (Numbers 11:33; 14:37). The Lord used these plagues to cause people to turn away from evil and back to God.

**❶ Avoid Pharaoh and similar global tyrants.**

Because Pharaoh and other kings tended to do greater evil than others, they enjoyed the distinction of receiving more plagues than normal people. Avoid keeping close company with such great evildoers.

**❷ Identify the sin.**

God sent plagues as a judgment because of specific sins. In the Bible these sins included enslaving a free nation, taking another man's wife, worshiping things other than God, and so on. If caught in a plague, identify what caused it. Once you've isolated the offending event, proceed to step three.

**❸** Repent.

To repent means to turn away from evil and back to God. Repenting involves praying to God, giving up specific evil actions in the short term, changing behavior in the long term, and receiving help from God. You cannot survive a plague on your own. The only way to survive a plague is through God's grace and the help God offers.

## Be Aware

- While the above steps will help ward off future plagues, surviving an ongoing one may require savvy specific to the situation at hand. Familiarize yourself with tactics associated with extreme hazard wilderness survival, medical first aid, and pest and disease control.

# TOP 10 PLAGUES OF THE OLD TESTAMENT

**1** Blood.

"[Moses] raised his staff in the presence of Pharaoh and his officials and struck the water of the Nile, and all the water was changed into blood."

*Exodus 7:20-21*

**2** Frogs.

"So Aaron stretched out his hand over the waters of Egypt, and the frogs came up and covered the land."

*Exodus 8:6*

**3** Gnats.

"They did this, and when Aaron stretched out his hand with the staff and struck the dust of the ground, gnats came upon men and animals. All the dust throughout the land of Egypt became gnats."

*Exodus 8:17*

**4** Flies.

"Dense swarms of flies poured into Pharaoh's palace and into the houses of his officials, and throughout Egypt the land was ruined by the flies."

*Exodus 8:24*

**5** Livestock plague.

"All the livestock of the Egyptians died, but not one animal belonging to the Israelites died."

*Exodus 9:6*

**6** Boils.

"So they took soot from a furnace and stood before Pharaoh. Moses tossed it into the air, and festering boils broke out on men and animals."

*Exodus 9:10*

**❼ Hail.**

"So the LORD rained hail on the land of Egypt; hail fell and lightning flashed back and forth. It was the worst storm in all the land of Egypt since it had become a nation."

*Exodus 9:23-24*

**❽ Locusts.**

"Never before had there been such a plague of locusts, nor will there ever be again. They covered all the ground until it was black."

*Exodus 10:14-15*

**❾ Darkness.**

"So Moses stretched out his hand toward the sky, and total darkness covered all Egypt for three days. No one could see anyone else or leave his place for three days."

*Exodus 10:22*

**❿ Death of the firstborn—Passover.**

"The blood will be a sign for you on the houses where you are; and when I see the blood, I will pass over you."

*Exodus 12:13*

"At midnight the LORD struck down all the firstborn in Egypt, from the firstborn of Pharaoh, who sat on the throne, to the firstborn of the prisoner, who was in the dungeon, and the firstborn of all the livestock as well."

*Exodus 12:29*

# THE THREE MOST REBELLIOUS THINGS JESUS DID

**❶ The prophet returned to his hometown (Luke 4:14-27).**
Jesus returned to Nazareth, where he was raised, and was invited to read Scripture and preach. First, he insisted that the scriptures he read were not just comforting promises of a distant future, but that they were about him, local boy, anointed by God. Second, he insisted God would bless foreigners with those same promises through him. These statements amounted to the unpardonable crime of blasphemy!

**❷ The rebel thumbed his nose at the authorities (John 11:55—12:11).**
Jesus had become an outlaw, hunted by the religious authorities who wanted to kill him. Mary, Martha, and Lazarus threw a thank-you party for Jesus in Bethany, right outside Jerusalem, the authorities' stronghold. In spite of the threats to his life, Jesus went to the party. This was not just rebellion but a demonstration of how much Jesus loved his friends.

**❸ The king rode a royal procession right under Caesar's nose (Matthew 21:1-17; Mark 11:1-10; Luke 19:28-38; John 12:12-19).**
Jesus entered Jerusalem during a great festival, in full view of adoring crowds, as a king come home to rule. Riding the colt, heralded by the people with cloaks and branches, accompanied by the royal anthem (Psalm 118), he rode in to claim Jerusalem for God and himself as God's anointed. The Roman overlords and the Jewish leaders watched this seditious act and prepared for a crucifixion.

# THREE THINGS WE KNOW ABOUT JESUS' CHILDHOOD

**❶ Jesus was born on earth as a human infant.**
This seemingly obvious point has profound implications. Jesus would later proclaim himself one with God. This means that God—who could have revealed himself to humankind in any form—chose the flesh, and came as a baby, totally dependent on parental nurturance and guidance. Consider this as a poetic mirror of the relationship we have with God.

**❷ He was an obedient child.**
The Bible says little about Jesus' childhood. Luke 2:51-52 states vaguely that "Jesus grew in wisdom and stature, and in favor with God and men." But that same passage also suggests that he was obedient to his parents. Not only is obedience a valuable quality for children, but here we get a glimpse into Jesus' character. Obedience is the very trait that defines his decision to take up the cross.

**❸ Jesus had siblings.**
Four brothers, according to Matthew 13:55 (James, Joses, Simon, and Judas—a different Judas from the disciple who betrayed Jesus). He also had sisters, though Matthew doesn't mention how many or what their names were. Jesus is believed to have been the oldest, because his mother was a virgin when he was conceived.

James
Joses
Simon
Judas

*Jesus had four brothers and probably some sisters.*

## Be Aware

- Other accounts of Jesus' childhood can be found in books NOT in the Bible, such as the Gospel of Thomas, but there is no way to verify their accuracy.

- For example, one story tells of Jesus playing at a brook while some other children stood watching. Jesus formed some handfuls of river clay into sparrows and arranged them on the bank. But it was the Sabbath, and another child reported to the adults that Jesus had been playing on the Sabbath. When Joseph came and asked Jesus why he wasn't keeping the law, Jesus clapped his hands and immediately the sparrows flew away chirping.

*One apocryphal story claims Jesus caused clay sparrows to come to life. Apocryphal means "of doubtful authenticity."*

- Another story claims that Jesus was playing in the upstairs of a house with another child who suddenly fell through the roof and died. Jesus, falsely accused of pushing him, then went to the body and told the child to rise, which he did.

- In yet another story, Jesus went to sow wheat with his father. He produced so much that he was able to give enough wheat to all the poor people in the village.

*Note:* These apocryphal stories should be regarded as interesting and entertaining—but unverifiable *and* extracanonical—anecdotes. The Bible clearly shows a predisposition for focusing on Jesus' life and ministry as an adult, along with his death and resurrection.

# THE SEVEN FUNNIEST BIBLE STORIES

Humor isn't scarce in the Bible; you just have to look for it. For example, God tells Abraham (100 years old) and Sarah (in her 90s) they'll soon have a son. Understandably, they laugh. Later, they have a son named Isaac, which means "he laughs." Bible humor is also ironic, gross, and sometimes just plain bizarre.

**❶ Gideon's dog-men (Judges 6:11—7:23).**
God chooses Gideon to lead an army against the Midianites. Gideon gathers an army of 32,000 men, but this is too many. God tells Gideon to make all the men drink from a stream, and then selects only the 300 men who lap water like dogs.

**❷ David ambushes Saul in a cave while he's "busy" (1 Samuel 24:2-7).**
While pursuing David cross-country to engage him in battle, Saul goes into a cave to "relieve himself" (move his bowels). Unbeknownst to Saul, David and his men are already hiding in the very same cave. While Saul's doing his business, David sneaks up and cuts off a corner of Saul's cloak with a knife. Outside afterward, David shows King Saul the piece of cloth to prove he could have killed him "on the throne."

**❸ King David does the goofy (2 Samuel 12-23).**
David is so excited about bringing the Ark of the Covenant to Jerusalem that he dances before God and all the people dressed only in a linen ephod, an apron-like garment that covered only the front of his body.

The doomed city of Sodom

*Lot's wife ignored God's warning. She looked back at the city of Sodom and became a pillar of salt.*

Pillar of salt
(formerly Lot's wife)

④ Lot's wife (Genesis 19:24-26).

While fleeing God's wrath upon the cities of Sodom and Gomorrah, Lot's wife forgets (or ignores) God's warning not to look back upon the destruction and turns into a woman-sized pillar of salt.

⑤ Gerasene demoniac (Mark 5:1-20).

A man is possessed by so many demons that chains cannot hold him. Jesus exorcises the demons and sends them into a herd of 2,000 pigs, which then run over the edge of a cliff and drown in the sea. The herders, now 2,000 pigs poorer, get miffed and ask Jesus to leave.

**6** Disciples and loaves of bread (Mark 8:14-21).
The disciples were there when Jesus fed 5,000 people
with just five loaves of bread and two fish. They also
saw him feed 4,000 people with seven loaves. Later, in a
boat, the disciples fret to an exasperated Jesus because
they have only one loaf for 13 people.

**7** Peter can't swim (Matthew 14:22-33).
Blundering Peter sees Jesus walking on the water and
wants to join him. But when the wind picks up,
Peter panics and starts to sink. In Greek, the name
Peter means "rock."

*Peter, "the rock,"
sank when he looked
to himself instead of
to Jesus. Jesus later
described Peter as a
Rock of the church
(Matthew 16:18).*

# THE FIVE GROSSEST BIBLE STORIES

**❶ Eglon and Ehud (Judges 3:12-30).**
Before kings reigned over Israel, judges ruled the people. At that time, a very overweight king named Eglon conquered Israel and demanded money. A man named Ehud brought the payment to Eglon while he was perched on his "throne" (meaning "toilet"). Along with the money, Ehud handed over a little something extra—his sword, which he buried so far in Eglon's belly that the sword disappeared into the king's fat and, as the Bible says, the dirt came out (v. 22).

**❷ Job's sores (Job 2:1-10).**
Job lived a righteous life yet he suffered anyway. He had oozing sores from the bald spot on top of his head clear down to the soft spot on the bottom of his foot. Job used a broken piece of pottery to scrape away the pus that leaked from his sores.

**❸ The naked prophet (Isaiah 20).**
God's prophets went to great lengths to get God's message across to the people. Isaiah was no exception. God's people planned a war, but God gave it the thumbs down. Isaiah marched around Jerusalem naked *for three years* as a sign of what would happen if the people went to war.

*Jeremiah strapped on some filthy underwear to show God could no longer be proud of the people.*

Filthy underwear

❹ **The almost-naked prophet (Jeremiah 13:1-11).**
God sent Jeremiah to announce that God could no longer be proud of the people. To make the point, Jeremiah bought a new pair of underclothes, wore them every day without washing them, then buried them in the wet river sand. Later, he dug them up, strapped them on, and shouted that this is what had happened to the people who were God's pride!

❺ **Spilling your guts (Matthew 27:1-8; Acts 1:16-19).**
Judas betrayed Jesus and sold him out for 30 pieces of silver. He bought a field with the ill-gotten loot. Guilt-stricken, Judas walked out to the field, his belly swelled up until it burst, and his intestines spilled out onto the ground.

# FIVE FACTS ABOUT LIFE IN OLD TESTAMENT TIMES

**1** Almost everyone wore sandals.
They were called "sandals" because people walked on sand much of the time.

**2** There were no newspapers.
People got news by hearing it from other people. Spreading important news was like a giant game of "telephone."

**3** It was dark.
Homes, often tents, were typically lit at night by an oil lamp, if at all.

**4** You had to fetch your water, which was scarce.
Rich folks had servants to carry it for them, but most people had to carry household water in jugs or leather bags, usually some distance, from a river or well.

**5** Life expectancy was short.
Despite some long-lived exceptions described in the book of Genesis, such as Abraham (175 years) and Methuselah (969 years), few people lived past 50.

*Sandals were made for walking on sand.*

# TEN IMPORTANT THINGS THAT HAPPENED BETWEEN THE OLD AND NEW TESTAMENTS

The period of time described in the Old Testament ended about 400 years before Jesus' birth. The people of God kept living, believing, struggling, and writing during that period. Here are some of the important events that took place between the Testaments.

**❶ The Hebrew nation dissolved.**
In 587 B.C., the Babylonians destroyed Jerusalem and Solomon's temple, and took the people into exile. Judah was never again an independent kingdom.

**❷ The people scattered.**
After the exile to Babylon ended, the people of Judah moved to many different places. Some of them later came back, but many never did. Some of them lived in Babylon, some lived in Egypt, and some just scattered elsewhere.

**❸ A religion replaced a nation.**
As a result of items 1 and 2, the people's religion changed. They no longer had a state or national religion (Judean religion). Instead, they had a freestanding faith called Judaism.

**❹ The Aramaic language became popular.**
Because Aramaic was the international language of the Persian Empire, many Jews quit speaking Hebrew and spoke Aramaic instead. This is why Jesus spoke Aramaic.

**⑤ Alexander the Great conquered the world.**
Around 330 B.C., Alexander the Great conquered the Mediterranean and Mesopotamian world. As a result, Greek became the everyday language of business and trade in the region. This is why the New Testament was written in Greek.

**⑥ The hammer dropped.**
Around 170 B.C., the Seleucid emperor outlawed circumcision and the Sabbath, and defiled the temple. A family of Jews called the Maccabees (which means "hammer") led a revolt.

*The Hebrew Scriptures were finally finished during the time between the Old and New Testaments.*

**7** **The Hebrew Scriptures were finished.**
During this time, the individual books that make up what we call the Old Testament were finished. Several other religious books written at this time (mostly in Greek) aren't in the Protestant Bible but are part of the Apocrypha.

**8** **The Sadducees, Pharisees, Essenes, Samaritans, Zealots, and other groups of people sprouted up.**
Different schools of thought developed within Judaism. Most of their disagreements were over the idea that God's people would be resurrected to eternal life.

**9** **God seemed to have forgotten the promise.**
God promised King David that one of his descendants would always be king in Jerusalem. But after the Babylonian exile, there were no kings in Jerusalem. People wondered what had happened to God's promise.

**10** **The Roman Empire expanded.**
In 63 B.C., the Roman Empire conquered Palestine, having already conquered pretty much everyone else in the region. This is why the Roman Empire ruled the area during the time of Jesus and the New Testament.

# FIVE FACTS ABOUT LIFE IN NEW TESTAMENT TIMES

**1** **Synagogues were not always buildings.**
For worship, Jesus' people gathered in all kinds of places, often outdoors. "Church" was any gathering of people for worship.

**2** **Houses were boxy.**
Most houses had a flat roof with an outside staircase leading to it. Inhabitants would sleep on the roof during hot weather.

**3** **Every town had a marketplace.**
Usually there was just one marketplace per town, but one could buy almost everything needed to live.

**4** **People ate a lot of fish.**
The most common fish in the Sea of Galilee were catfish and carp. Roasting over a charcoal fire was the most common method of cooking.

**5** **Dogs were shunned.**
The Jewish people in Jesus' day did not keep dogs as pets. Dogs were considered unclean because they ate garbage and animal carcasses.

*Houses in New Testament times were boxy.*

# JESUS' TWELVE APOSTLES (PLUS MATTHIAS AND PAUL)

While Jesus had many disciples (students and followers) the Bible focuses particularly on twelve who were closest to him. Tradition says that these twelve spread Jesus' message throughout the known world (Matthew 28:18-20). For this reason, they were known as *apostles*, a word that means "sent ones."

**❶ Andrew.**

A fisherman and the first disciple to follow Jesus, Andrew brought his brother, Simon Peter, to Jesus.

**❷ Bartholomew.**

Also called Nathanael, tradition has it that he was martyred by being skinned alive.

**❸ James the Elder.**

James, with John and Peter, was one of Jesus' closest disciples. Herod Agrippa killed James because of his faith, which made him a martyr (Acts 12:2).

**❹ John.**

John (or one of his followers) is thought to be the author of the Gospel of John and three Letters of John. He probably died of natural causes in old age.

**❺ Matthew.**

Matthew was a tax collector and, therefore, probably an outcast even among his own people. He is attributed with the authorship of the Gospel of Matthew.

**6** Peter.

Peter was a fisherman who was brought to faith by his brother Andrew. He was probably martyred in Rome by being crucified upside down.

**7** Philip.

Philip, possibly a Greek, is responsible for bringing Bartholomew (Nathanael) to faith. He is thought to have died in a city called Phrygia.

**8** James the Less.

This James was called "the Less" so he wouldn't be confused with James, the brother of John—or with James, Jesus' brother.

**9** Simon.

Simon is often called "the Zealot." Zealots were a political group in Jesus' day that favored the overthrow of the Roman government by force.

**10** Jude.

Jude may have worked with Simon the Zealot in Persia (Iran) where they were martyred on the same day.

**11** Thomas.

"Doubting" Thomas preached the message of Jesus in India.

**12** Judas Iscariot.

Judas was the treasurer for Jesus' disciples and the one who betrayed Jesus for 30 pieces of silver. According to the Bible, Judas killed himself for his betrayal.

**⑬ Matthias.**

Matthias was chosen by lot to replace Judas. It is thought that he worked mostly in Ethiopia.

**⑭ Paul.**

Paul is considered primarily responsible for bringing non-Jewish people to faith in Jesus. He traveled extensively and wrote many letters to believers. Many of Paul's letters are included in the New Testament.

# THE FIVE WEIRDEST LAWS IN THE OLD TESTAMENT

The Old Testament has many helpful, common sense laws, such as "You shall not kill," and, "You shall not steal." But there are a few others that need some explaining.

**❶ The "ox" law.**
"If a bull gores a man or a woman to death, the bull must be stoned to death, and its meat must not be eaten. But the owner of the bull will not be held responsible" (Exodus 21:28). Replace "bull" with "car" and the law makes more sense—it is about protecting others from reckless actions.

*People living in biblical times were sometimes gored by bulls.*

*People who were gored by bulls—or victims of other crimes—had legal recourse.*

**❷ The "no kid boiling" law.**
"Do not cook a young goat in its mother's milk" (Exodus 23:19b). A "kid," of course, is a juvenile goat, not a human being.

**❸ The "which bugs are legal to eat" law.**
"All flying insects that walk on all fours are to be detestable to you. There are, however, some winged creatures that walk on all fours that you may eat" (Leviticus 11:20-21). The law is unclear whether it is legal to eat the bug if you first pull off the legs.

**❹ The "don't eat blood" law.**
"None of you may eat blood" (Leviticus 17:12). Some laws beg the question whether people in that time had any sense of taste.

**❺ The "pure cloth" law.**
"Do not wear clothes of wool and linen woven together" (Deuteronomy 22:11). Polyester came along after Bible times.

# THE TOP 10 BIBLE MIRACLES AND WHAT THEY MEAN

**1** Creation.

God created the universe and everything that is in it, and God continues to create and recreate without ceasing. God's first and ongoing miracle was to reveal that the creation has a purpose.

**2** The Passover.

The Israelites were enslaved by Pharaoh, a ruler who believed the people belonged to him, not to God. In the last of 10 plagues, God visited the houses of all the Egyptians to kill the firstborn male in each one. God alone is Lord of the people, and no human can claim ultimate power over us.

**3** The Exodus.

God's people were fleeing Egypt when Pharaoh dispatched his army to force them back into slavery. The army trapped the people with their backs to a sea, but God parted the water and the people walked across to freedom while Pharaoh's minions were destroyed. God chose to free us from all forms of tyranny so we may use that freedom to serve God and each other.

**4** Manna.

After the people crossed the sea to freedom, they complained that they were going to starve to death. They even asked to go back to Egypt. God sent manna, a form of bread, so the people lived. God cares for us even when we give up, pine for our slavery, and lose faith. God never abandons us.

**⑤ The Incarnation.**
The immortal and infinite God became a human being, choosing to be born of a woman. God loved us enough to become one of us in Jesus of Nazareth, forever bridging the divide that had separated us from God.

**⑥ Jesus healed the paralyzed man.**
Some men brought a paralyzed friend to Jesus. Jesus said, "Son, your sins are forgiven" (Mark 2:5). This means that Jesus has the power to forgive our sins—and he does so as a free gift.

**⑦ Jesus calmed the storm.**
Jesus was asleep in a boat with his disciples when a great storm came up and threatened to sink it. He said, "Quiet! Be still!" (Mark 4:39). Then the storm immediately calmed. Jesus is Lord over even the powers of nature.

**⑧ The Resurrection.**
Human beings executed Jesus, but God raised him from the dead on the third day. Through baptism, we share in Jesus' death, so we will also share in eternal life with God the Father, Son, and Holy Spirit. Christ conquered death.

**⑨ Pentecost.**
Jesus ascended from the earth, but he did not leave the church powerless or alone. On the 50th day after the Jewish Passover (*Pentecost* means 50th), Jesus sent the Holy Spirit to create the church and take up residence among us. The Holy Spirit is present with us always.

**⑩ The Second Coming.**
One day, Christ will come again and end all suffering. This means that the final result of the epic battle between good and evil is already assured. It is simply that evil has not yet admitted defeat.

# THE LORD'S PRAYER

## Scriptural Version

Our Father in heaven,
hallowed be your name,
your kingdom come,
your will be done
on earth as it is in heaven.
Give us today our daily bread.
Forgive us our debts,
as we also have forgiven our debtors.
And lead us not into temptation,
but deliver us from the evil one.

*Matthew 6:9-13*

## Modern Version

Our Father in heaven,
  hallowed be your name,
  your kingdom come,
  your will be done,
    on earth as in heaven.
Give us today our daily bread.
Forgive us our sins*
  as we forgive those
    who sin* against us.
Save us from the time of trial
  and deliver us from evil.[+]
For the kingdom, the power,
  and the glory are yours,
  now and forever. Amen

* Other versions use "debts" and "debtors" here.

## Traditional Version

Our Father, who art in heaven,
   hallowed by thy name,
   thy kingdom come,
   thy will be done,
   on earth as it is in heaven.
Give us this day our daily bread;
and forgive us our trespasses,*
   as we forgive those
   who trespass* against us;
and lead us not into temptation,
   but deliver us from evil.+
For thine is the kingdom,
   and the power, and the glory,
   forever and ever. Amen

+ Other versions use "the evil one" here.

# THE TEN COMMANDMENTS

1.  I am the LORD your God, who brought you out of Egypt, out of the land of slavery. You shall have no other gods before me.

2.  You shall not make for yourself an idol in the form of anything in heaven above or on the earth beneath or in the waters below.

3.  You shall not misuse the name of the LORD your God, for the LORD will not hold anyone guiltless who misuses his name.

4.  Remember the Sabbath day by keeping it holy.

5.  Honor your father and your mother, so that you may live long in the land the LORD your God is giving you.

6.  You shall not murder.

7.  You shall not commit adultery.

8.  You shall not steal.

9.  You shall not give false testimony against your neighbor.

10. You shall not covet your neighbor's house. You shall not covet your neighbor's wife, or his manservant or maidservant, his ox or donkey, or anything that belongs to your neighbor.

*Exodus 20:1-17*

# THE EXODUS

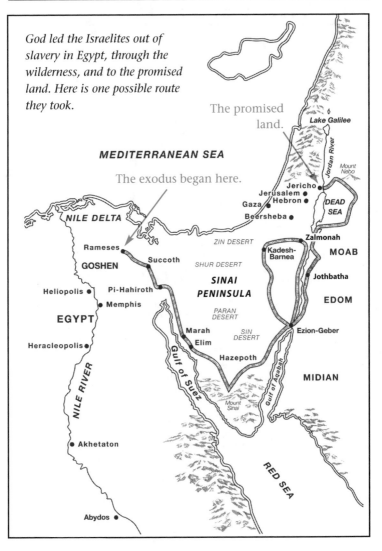

God led the Israelites out of slavery in Egypt, through the wilderness, and to the promised land. Here is one possible route they took.

The promised land.

Lake Galilee

The exodus began here.

MEDITERRANEAN SEA

Jordan River

Mount Nebo

Jericho
Jerusalem
Gaza    Hebron
Beersheba

DEAD SEA

NILE DELTA

ZIN DESERT

Zalmonah

Rameses

Succoth

SHUR DESERT

Kadesh-Barnea

MOAB

GOSHEN

SINAI PENINSULA

Jothbatha

Heliopolis

Pi-Hahiroth

Memphis

PARAN DESERT

EDOM

EGYPT

Marah
Elim

SIN DESERT

Ezion-Geber

Heracleopolis

Hazepoth

MIDIAN

Gulf of Suez

Gulf of Aqabah

Mount Sinai

NILE RIVER

Akhetaton

RED SEA

Abydos

# THE HOLY LAND—
# OLD TESTAMENT TIMES

# THE HOLY LAND—
# NEW TESTAMENT TIMES

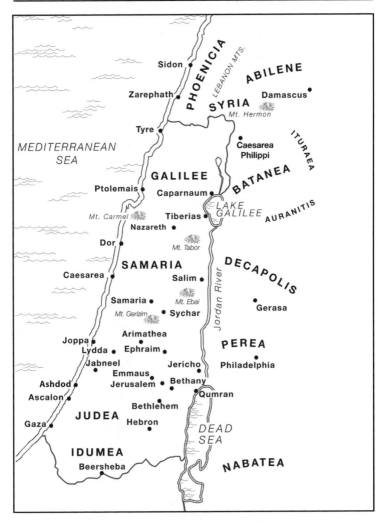

MEDITERRANEAN
SEA

PHOENICIA
LEBANON MTS.
ABILENE
Sidon
Zarephath
Damascus
SYRIA
Mt. Hermon
Tyre
Caesarea
Philippi
ITURAEA
GALILEE
BATANEA
Ptolemais
Caparnaum
LAKE
GALILEE
AURANITIS
Mt. Carmel
Tiberias
Nazareth
Dor
Mt. Tabor
DECAPOLIS
SAMARIA
Caesarea
Salim
Jordan River
Samaria
Mt. Ebai
Mt. Gerizim
Sychar
Gerasa
Arimathea
Joppa
Lydda
Ephraim
PEREA
Jabneel
Jericho
Philadelphia
Emmaus
Ashdod
Jerusalem
Bethany
Ascalon
Qumran
Bethlehem
Gaza
JUDEA
Hebron
DEAD
SEA
IDUMEA
Beersheba
NABATEA

# THE ROMAN EMPIRE DURING JESUS' TIME

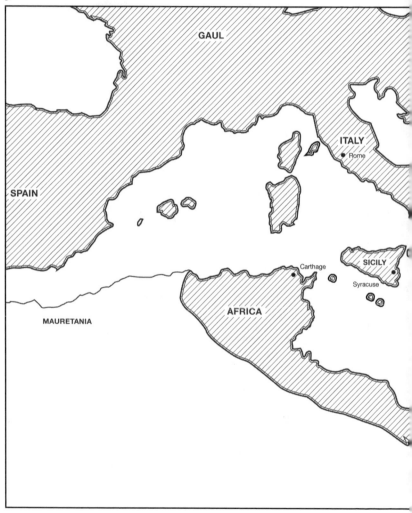

# PAUL'S JOURNEYS

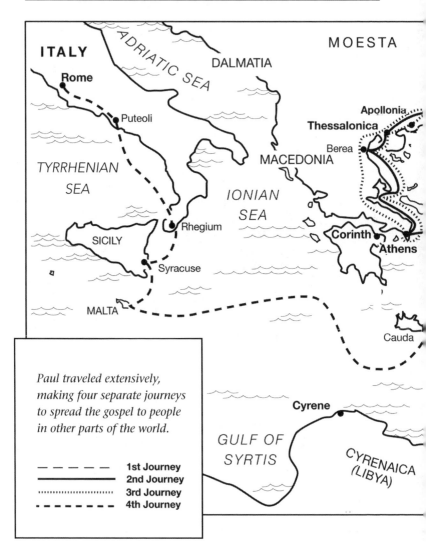

Paul traveled extensively, making four separate journeys to spread the gospel to people in other parts of the world.

| | |
|---|---|
| – – – – – | 1st Journey |
| ———— | 2nd Journey |
| ············· | 3rd Journey |
| –  –  –  – | 4th Journey |

THRACE

BLACK SEA

**Philippi**

Neapolis

**Byzantium**

ASIA

GALATIA

CAPPADOCIA

Troas

LYDIA

**Pisidian Antioch**

**Iconium**

CHIOS

**Ephesus**

**Sardis**

Colossae

**Lystra**

Derbe

**Tarsus**

SAMOS

Miletus

Cnidus

Attalia

Perga

Cos

**Myra**

Patara

Seleucia

CRETE

Salamis

Casea

**CYPRUS**

MEDITERRANEAN SEA

**Sidon**

**Tyre**

Ptolemais

**Caesarea**

**Alexandria**

**Jerusalem**

*DEAD SEA*

EGYPT

0          300 mi.

0          400 km.

# JERUSALEM IN JESUS' TIME

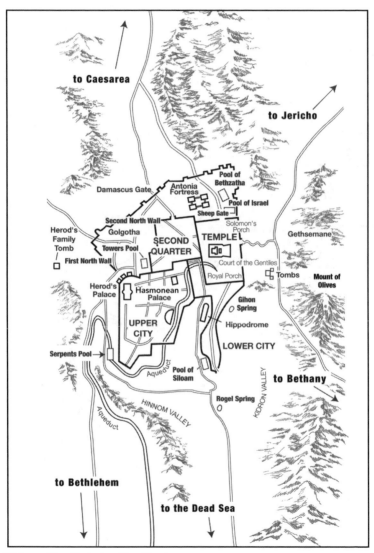

to Caesarea

to Jericho

Damascus Gate

Pool of Bethzatha

Antonia Fortress

Pool of Israel

Sheep Gate

Second North Wall

Solomon's Porch

Golgotha

Herod's Family Tomb

SECOND QUARTER

TEMPLE

Gethsemane

Towers Pool

First North Wall

Court of the Gentiles

Royal Porch

Tombs

Mount of Olives

Herod's Palace

Hasmonean Palace

Gihon Spring

UPPER CITY

Hippodrome

LOWER CITY

Serpents Pool

Aqueduct

Pool of Siloam

KIDRON VALLEY

to Bethany

HINNOM VALLEY

Rogel Spring

Aqueduct

to Bethlehem

to the Dead Sea

# NOAH'S ARK

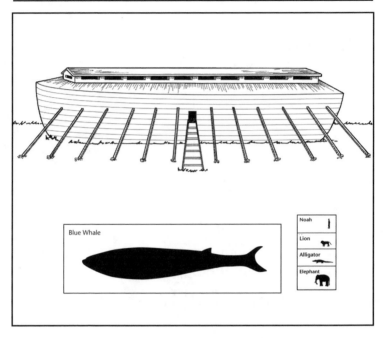

Blue Whale

Noah
Lion
Alligator
Elephant

A cubit is equal to the length of a man's forearm from the elbow to the tip of the middle finger—approximately 18 inches or 45.7 centimeters. Noah's ark was 300 cubits long, 50 cubits wide, and 30 cubits tall (Genesis 6:15).

One Cubit

# THE TOWER OF BABEL

**Genesis 11**

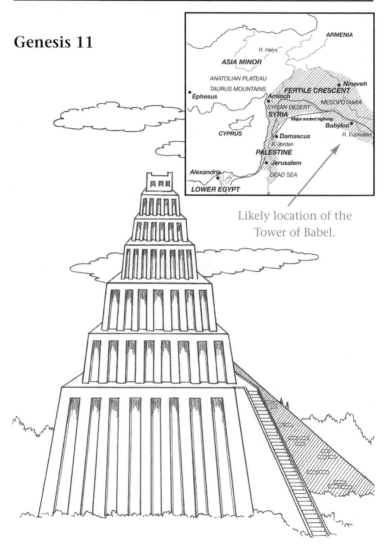

Likely location of the Tower of Babel.

# THE BURNING BUSH

## Exodus 3:2

Moses

Bush afire but not consumed.

# THE ARK OF THE COVENANT

*God told the Israelites to place the stone tablets—the "covenant"—of the law into the Ark of the Covenant. The Israelites believed that God was invisibly enthroned above the vessel and went before them wherever they traveled.*

*The Ark of the Covenant was 2.5 cubits long and 1.5 cubits wide (Exodus 25:17).*

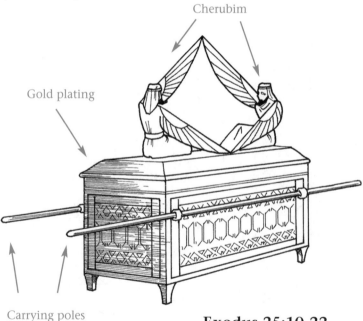

Cherubim

Gold plating

Carrying poles

**Exodus 25:10-22**

# SOLOMON'S TEMPLE

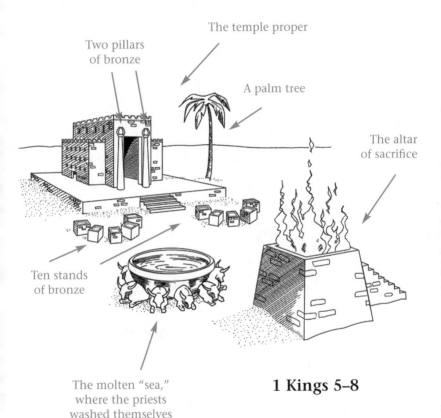

The temple proper

Two pillars
of bronze

A palm tree

The altar
of sacrifice

Ten stands
of bronze

The molten "sea,"
where the priests
washed themselves

**1 Kings 5–8**

# SOLOMON'S TEMPLE (FLOOR PLAN)

**1 Kings 8**

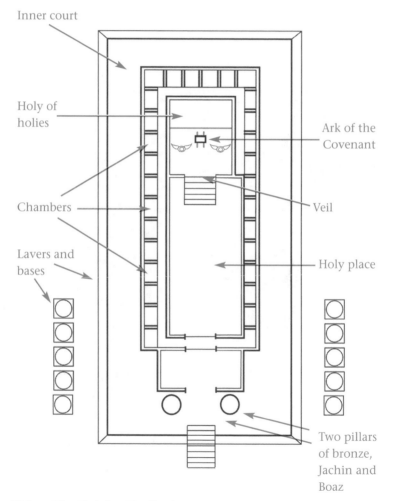

Inner court

Holy of holies

Ark of the Covenant

Chambers

Veil

Lavers and bases

Holy place

Two pillars of bronze, Jachin and Boaz

# THE ARMOR OF GOD

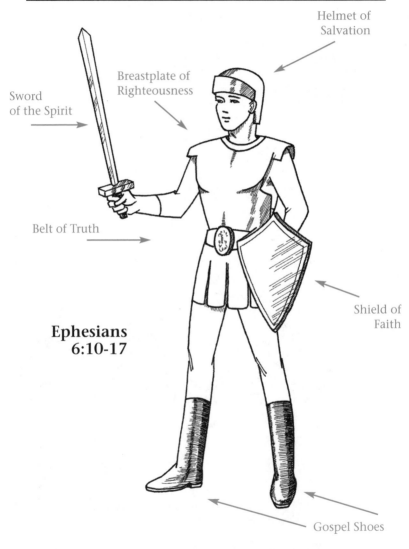

Helmet of Salvation

Breastplate of Righteousness

Sword of the Spirit

Belt of Truth

Shield of Faith

**Ephesians 6:10-17**

Gospel Shoes

# THE PASSION AND CRUCIFIXION

*Judas betrayed Jesus with a kiss, saying, "the one I will kiss is the man; arrest him" (Matthew 26:48).*

*Peter denied Jesus three times (Matthew 26:69-75).*

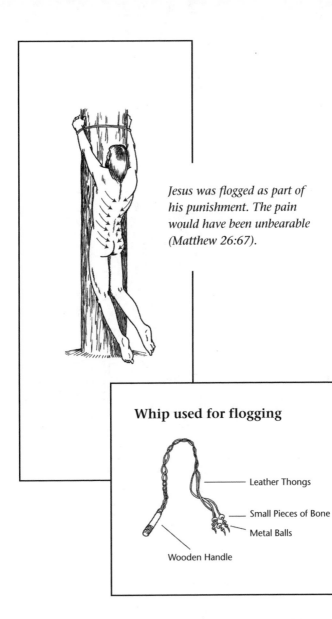

*Jesus was flogged as part of his punishment. The pain would have been unbearable (Matthew 26:67).*

## Whip used for flogging

Leather Thongs

Small Pieces of Bone

Metal Balls

Wooden Handle

*After being flogged, carrying the patibulum was nearly impossible for Jesus.*

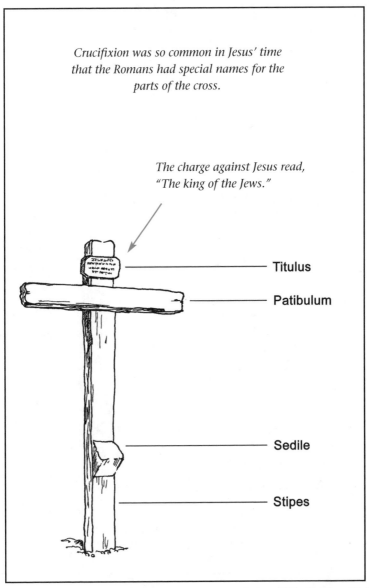

Crucifixion was so common in Jesus' time that the Romans had special names for the parts of the cross.

The charge against Jesus read, "The king of the Jews."

Titulus

Patibulum

Sedile

Stipes

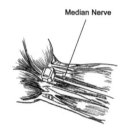

Median Nerve

*Typical crucifixion involved being nailed to the cross through the wrists— an excruciatingly painful and humiliating punishment.*

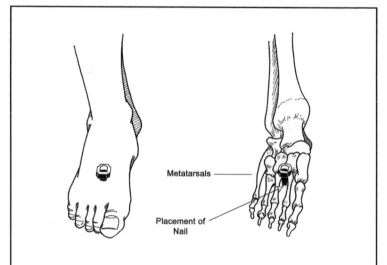

Metatarsals

Placement of Nail

*During a crucifixion, a single nail usually was used to pin both feet together to the cross.*

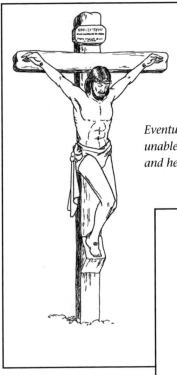

*Eventually, the victim would be unable to lift himself to take a breath, and he would suffocate.*

*While the Romans broke the legs of the men who were crucified next to Jesus, they found that Jesus had already died. To make sure, they pierced his side with a spear, probably to puncture his heart (John 19:34).*

## Jesus' Seven Sayings on the Cross

1. "Father, forgive them, for they do not know what they are doing." *Luke 23:34*

2. "I tell you the truth, today you will be with me in paradise." *Luke 23:43*

3. To his mother: "Dear woman, here is your son."
   To the disciple John: "Here is your mother." *John 19:26-27*

4. *"Eloi, Eloi, lama sabachthani?"* which means, "My God, my God, why have you forsaken me?" *Matthew 27:46*

5. "I am thirsty." *John 19:28*

6. "It is finished." *John 19:30*

7. "Father, into your hands I commit my spirit."
   When he had said this, he breathed his last. *Luke 23:46*

*Joseph of Arimathea and several women took Jesus down and carried him to the tomb (Matthew 27:57-61).*

*The miracle of resurrection took place three days later, when Jesus rose from the dead.*

# JESUS' FAMILY TREE

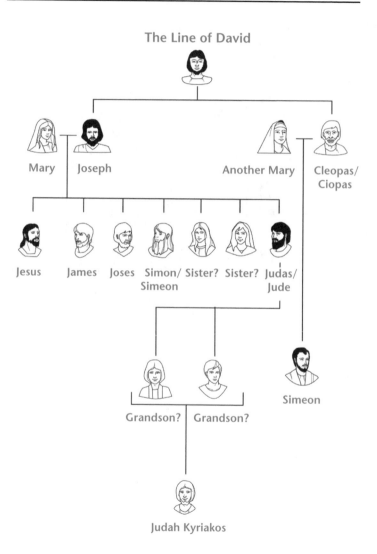

The Line of David

Mary  Joseph                    Another Mary  Cleopas/
                                              Ciopas

Jesus  James  Joses  Simon/  Sister?  Sister?  Judas/
                     Simeon                    Jude

Grandson?  Grandson?          Simeon

Judah Kyriakos

# COMMON CHRISTIAN SYMBOLS AND WHAT THEY MEAN

## Crosses

Greek Cross: This form is distinguished by its four equal arms.

Latin Cross: The Latin cross, the traditional cross of Jesus' crucifixion, always has the lower vertical arm longer than any other. Sometimes the upper arm is shorter than, sometimes equal to, the horizontal arms.

Tau Cross: This form receives its name from the letter "T" ("Tau" in Greek), which is shaped this way in Greek and Latin. According to one tradition, St. Philip was martyred on such a cross.

St. Andrew's Cross: The name derives from a tradition that states that St. Andrew was martyred on a cross of this form.

Double Cross: This form results from a Latin cross on which the Board of Inscription, the title placed over Jesus at his crucifixion, has been attached.

Byzantine or Russian Cross: Frequently used in Byzantine art, this form is the Double Cross with the addition of a footrest.

Forked Cross: Known in the Middle Ages as a "thief's cross," this form suggests overtones of the Trinity. For some it stresses the prayer aspects of Christ's suffering since the arms simulate arms lifted in prayer.

**Papal Cross:** This is a Double Cross with the addition of another horizontal arm.

**Ring Cross or Egyptian Cross:** In pre-Christian Egypt, this was the hieroglyphic sign for life. It was taken over by Coptic (Egyptian) Christians as the sign for true life. Some variations incorporate the Greek letters *alpha* and *omega* to emphasize Christ as the true beginning and ending.

**Multiple Cross:** This form results from the combination of four Latin crosses and suggests the four corners of the world over which Jesus reigns.

**Crutch Cross:** A form of the cross developed from four Tau crosses, each arm also resembling a crutch.

**Jerusalem Cross or Pilgrim's Cross:** The addition of four small crosses to a Greek cross suggests in sum the five wounds of Christ. It was a favorite emblem of 11th- and 12th-century pilgrims visiting Jerusalem.

**Maltese Cross:** This cross is distinguished by its eight points, which together mean fullness or completion.

**Anchor Cross:** This ancient variation of the cross is meant to convey hope and often is combined with the symbol of the fish.

**Staff Cross:** A cross at the end of a staff indicates authority, especially if it is jeweled or adorned with precious metals. Placed in an upright position, it conveys the authority of Christ's reign in a particular place or in the whole world.

## Four Evangelists

Matthew is depicted as a human or angel, because his Gospel stresses the genealogy and humanity of Christ.

Mark, represented by a lion, lifts up the royal divinity and resurrection of Jesus.

Luke, seen as an ox, accents the sacrificial nature of Jesus.

John, whose Gospel soars into the wisdom of God and mirrors the ascension, is presented as an eagle.

## Letters

ALPHA and OMEGA: In the Greek alphabet, *alpha* is the first letter, and *omega* is the last. Upper case forms are used most frequently as symbols for Jesus identified as the first and the last.

I/IOTA: In Greek the letter *iota* is the same as "I" and is the first letter of the name of Jesus.

T/TAU: This Greek letter is in the shape of a cross and therefore represents Christ and the crucifixion.

X/CHI: In the Greek alphabet, this letter is the first letter of the word for Christ. It is usually employed with other letters to form monograms.

# Monograms

**CHI-RHO:** *Chi* and *Rho* are the first two letters of the Greek word for Christ.

**CHI-IOTA:** *Chi* is the first letter of the Greek word for Christ, and *iota* is the first letter of the Greek word for Jesus.

**IC XC NIKA:** *Iota* with "C" is shorthand for the Greek word for Jesus. *Chi* with "C" or "S" denotes the Greek word for Christ. Both used with the Greek NIKA, which means "conquers," thus mean: "Jesus Christ conquers."

**ICHTHUS:** This is the Greek word for fish. As a monogram it originates from the first letters of five names for Jesus: *Iesus, Christos, Uios, Theos,* and *Soter.*

**IHS:** Another popular variation of the first letters of Jesus' name in Greek capitals is IHSOUS, IHS, or IHC, since "S" was sometimes written as "C."

**INRI:** These are the first letters of the four Latin words *Iesus Nazarenus Rex, Judaeorum* (Jesus of Nazareth, King of the Jews).

**SDG:** The first letters of the Latin words *Soli Deo Gloria* mean "To God alone be glory."

**AMDG:** These are the first letters of the four Latin words *Ad Majorem Dei Gloriam* ("To the greater glory of God"). The letters are frequently found inscribed on buildings or cornerstones.

# Geometric Figures

**Circle:** Because it has no point of beginning or ending, the circle is an image of eternity or fullness. The circle also elicits the notion of equality since every point is equidistant from the center. Wheels as moving circles indicate never-ending motion and have been employed to represent the course of the sun (God's Son), the year, and its seasons.

**Nimbus:** The Latin word *nimbus* means cloud, which is what people often imagine as surrounding the appearance of a godlike being. The nimbus appears as a circle, or halo, surrounding the head of a god or of a godlike person. Sometimes it is star-shaped, triangular (for God the Father), or rectangular (for someone still living). Three rays of light, or an equally segmented nimbus, sometimes surround a symbol of a person of the Trinity. A nimbus implies glory, which is why the color of a nimbus is usually white or gold. When a nimbus surrounds the entire figure representing God or a saint, it is called *aureole*, meaning "golden" or "glorious."

**Triangle:** A triangle with equal sides suggests the Trinity. Usually the triangle is depicted with other symbols, such as a circle, the eye of God, a hand, or a dove.

**Triquetra:** The triquetra, a symbol for the Trinity, is formed by three equal arcs that have been interwoven to suggest continuous flow. The points of the arcs are the points of an imagined equilateral triangle, another symbol of the Trinity.

# Animals

Butterfly: The butterfly is a symbol of the death and resurrection of Christ, and thus of any faithful Christian. In pre-Christian times, it was understood to be a symbol of the soul, deriving its meaning from the three stages of a butterfly's life: caterpillar (life), chrysalis (death), and butterfly (resurrection).

Cock/Hen: As the morning herald of light, the cock was an ancient symbol for the recurring victory of light over darkness. On weather vanes and peaks of church buildings, the cock is meant to summon the faithful to prayer and repentance. Crowing cocks thus are also symbols of the ministry. The hen derives its symbolic significance from Jesus' reference to himself as the hen who gathers the faithful.

Dove: The dove is the preeminent symbol for the Holy Spirit since, according to the evangelists, it was chosen to embody the Holy Spirit at Jesus' baptism. By extension the dove also symbolizes Pentecost. It is the means by which divine inspiration is depicted. Seven doves refer to the seven gifts of the Spirit. A dove with an olive branch in its mouth recalls Noah and the ark and is meant to convey peace and forgiveness.

Eagle: In pre-Christian cultures, people were convinced that eagles flew to the sun in order to find new life and strength for their wings. Hence, the eagle became a symbol for either life in Christ or for a Christian's personal ascension. As eagles take their young to the sun for fresh vistas of perception and understanding, so the eagle became a symbol for contemplation and discovery of the mysteries of God. St. John is represented by an eagle.

**Fish:** The fish was a common symbol for water. When combined with an anchor, it became a symbol of baptism for Christians. Because Jesus fed the hungry crowd with loaves and fish, which many Christians understood as a form of Holy Communion, the fish is sometimes employed as a symbol for Communion. *Ichthus*, the Greek word for fish, is composed of the initials of Jesus, Christ, God, Son, and Savior.

**Lamb:** Because of the Passover, the lamb and its blood have been recognized as signs of God's deliverance—later referring to Jesus, the Lamb of God, as the specific means of God's deliverance. The lamb, with a staff cross, frequently appears with the four evangelists. Lambs can also symbolize Christians gathered as the church, with Jesus as their Good Shepherd.

**Lion:** The lion connotes strength and potential destruction. The lion is viewed as a protector of graves and of cities, and sometimes is associated with the resurrection. In some Christian art, Christ as lion seeks to destroy the dragon or devil. The lion is the symbol for St. Mark.

**Ox:** The ox represents fruitfulness of the earth, presumably because of its use in tilling. In the Old Testament, young oxen offspring were often sacrificed in cultic rituals, which led to Christian use of the ox as a symbol of Christ's sacrifice. St. Luke, the evangelist, is represented by an ox.

**Phoenix:** The phoenix is a symbol for the resurrected Christ. In Egyptian tradition, the phoenix had a life span of nearly 500 years. Then, at the close of its life, the phoenix would fly to the Heliopolis and burn itself on a funeral pyre. After three days, it would rise from the ashes and return to its home.

**Snake/Dragon:** Because the serpent in the Genesis story of human temptation and the fall has been interpreted as a snake, a snake symbolizes temptation, evil, or the devil. Dragons, mythological beasts meant to induce terror, are often employed as substituted for or equivalents of snakes.

## Cosmic Elements

**Fire, Light, Candle:** Fire frequently accompanies an epiphany of God, such as in the burning bush. Light produced by fire is a symbol of the pervading presence of God because the light of Christ vanquishes the darkness of sin and death. The Holy Spirit was embodied in flames, so the Spirit or the seven gifts of the Spirit are represented often as flames. Hearts aflame denote burning love, especially for God. Fire is also a symbol of purification, so it is associated with the testing of saints.

**Wind:** Wind symbolizes the breath of God. Being felt, not seen, sometimes directional, sometimes absent, wind has a mysterious and unpredictable character. Specifically it is a symbol of the Holy Spirit.

**Sun, Light:** Christians took up the sun as a symbol for God; they faced east for prayer and built church buildings so worshipers could naturally look east in order to praise God. As Christians confessed Jesus to be God's Son, they thought of him also as the sun, but even more as the Light of the world.

**Moon and Stars:**

- *Moon:* Because the sun became darkened at the crucifixion, the sun and moon are sometimes chosen by artists to symbolize visually the effect of Jesus' death on all of creation. Sun and moon occasionally denote the Old and New Testaments, and also signal the destruction of the world. Because the phases of the moon include a "death," the moon also represents birth, death, and resurrection.

- *Stars:* Together with the sun and moon, the stars symbolize creation, especially creation's obedience to God since stars, it was thought, stayed where God put them. Stars also signify heaven in Christian art. A single bright star with a manger stands for the Star of Bethlehem and messianic fulfillment. Jesus the Messiah is known as the bright Morning Star. Seven stars refer to the angels of the seven congregations in Revelation. Twelve stars represent a crown for Mary, the heavenly woman, and a single star sometimes represents Mary as the Star of the Sea.

**Seasons:** In Christian symbolism the four seasons are represented by blooms (spring), grain (summer), grapes (fall), and olives or fire for warmth (winter).

# Implements

**Keys:** One or two keys, the symbol for power or status, represent the apostle Peter, since he and his colleagues received the authority to bind and loose sins on earth. Entrance to eternal life is via Jesus as the key himself.

**Staff:** A long staff is a tool or symbol of a shepherd. A staff with a crook symbolizes a spiritual shepherd. In ancient times, the staff meant protective power as well as authority to work miraculous deeds. Most often, Jesus is depicted as the Good Shepherd who holds the staff.

**Sword:** As an implement of battle and war, the sword denotes might. From might comes authority for making judgments. A two-edged sword stresses judgment and is meant to lift up Jesus the ultimate judge over life and death. Jesus carries out his task through the Word, both Law and Gospel, the two edges of the sword. The sword is also a symbol of martyrdom.

**Towel, Ewer (pitcher), Basin:** These three items have to do with washing and therefore symbolize cleanliness or purity. Opportunities for washing was offered to guests as a sign of hospitality. Jesus, washing the feet of his disciples, turned cleanliness into loving service. Hence, the towel, ewer (pitcher), and basin also symbolize ministry.

## Symbols of the Trinity

**God the Father:** This common symbol, showing God's blessing and protection, is formed by placing a hand within a circular nimbus.

**God the Son:** Five simple symbols have been used to form this symbol of Jesus: lamb, staff cross, nimbus, blood, and chalice. Together they express the sacrificial death of God's Son, Jesus.

**God the Spirit:** One of the most familiar symbols of the Holy Spirit combines the dove with the nimbus.

## Church

**Ship:** When a ship, a place of refuge, is portrayed with a mast shaped like a cross, it is usually understood to symbolize the Christian church. A ship with a rainbow recalls God's promises to Noah and his family, and God's deliverance through water and the ark.

# THE CHRISTIAN FLAG AND ITS HISTORY

## History

The idea for a Christian flag originated on September 26, 1897, in Brooklyn, New York, when Sunday school superintendent Charles C. Overton delivered an extemporaneous talk to students, because the scheduled speaker didn't show.

Using the U.S. flag as his inspiration, Overton asked the students what a flag representing the Christian faith might look like. A decade later, he and Ralph Diffendorfer, who was secretary of the Methodist Young People's Missionary Movement, codesigned and began promoting the flag.

## Meaning

The Christian flag takes its colors and basic design from the U.S. flag. The elements of the flag, however, represent purely Christian ideas, independent of any nation or state.

- The strongest symbol is the cross, the universal symbol for Jesus Christ.

- The red color evokes an image of his blood and calls to mind his crucifixion. Christians believe Jesus' death and resurrection are the means God uses to save all people from their sins.

- The white background draws from passages throughout the Bible that connect the color white with purity, forgiveness, and the presence of God. People who have been "washed white as snow" (Isaiah 1:18) have been cleansed of their sins.

- The meaning of the blue canton, though historically uncertain, has been interpreted to represent heaven, truth, and the rite of Baptism in water.

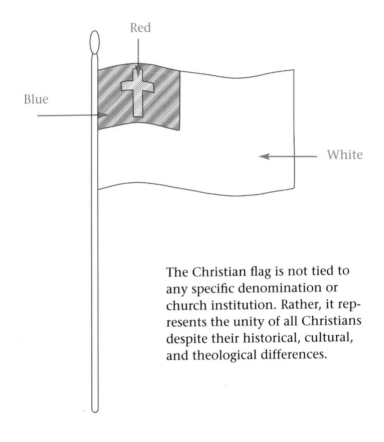

Red

Blue

White

The Christian flag is not tied to any specific denomination or church institution. Rather, it represents the unity of all Christians despite their historical, cultural, and theological differences.

# LIST OF CONTRIBUTORS

### Editor

Kristofer Skrade has pastored congregations in Seattle and St. Paul, and currently serves as New Brand Development Editor at Augsburg Fortress, Publishers. He lives in St. Paul, Minnesota, with his wife, Ivy.

### Reviewers

Kirk Livingston

Richard Webb

### *Contributors*

Lou Carlozo

Mark Gardner

Wes Halula

Sarah Henrich

Mark Hinton

Sue Houglum

Rolf Jacobson

Susan M. Lang

Andrea Lee

Daniel Levitin

Kirk Livingston

Catherine Malotky

Terry Marks

Jeffrey S. Nelson

Rebecca Ninke

Dawn Rundman

Jonathan Rundman

Ken Sundet Jones

Hans Wiersma